Multicultural Education in an Age of Globalization

Multicultural Education in an Age of Globalization

Compelling Issues for Engagement

Chinaka Samuel DomNwachukwu

ROWMAN & LITTLEFIELD
Lanham • Boulder • New York • London

Published by Rowman & Littlefield
An imprint of The Rowman & Littlefield Publishing Group, Inc.
4501 Forbes Boulevard, Suite 200, Lanham, Maryland 20706
www.rowman.com

6 Tinworth Street, London SE11 5AL, United Kingdom

Copyright © 2019 by Chinaka Samuel DomNwachukwu

All rights reserved. No part of this book may be reproduced in any form or by any electronic or mechanical means, including information storage and retrieval systems, without written permission from the publisher, except by a reviewer who may quote passages in a review.

British Library Cataloguing in Publication Information Available

Library of Congress Cataloging-in-Publication Data Available

ISBN: 978-1-4758-1886-4 (cloth)
ISBN: 978-1-4758-1887-1 (pbk.)
ISBN: 978-1-4758-1888-8 (electronic)

Contents

Introduction		vii
1	From Colonialism to a Global Community	1
2	Globalization and Multiculturalism	19
3	Federal Affirmative Action and Its Implications for Equal Educational Opportunities in the United States	33
4	Global Issues on Gender Equity	47
5	The Advancement of Gender Equity in the United States	71
6	Religious Diversity and the Public School Systems	85
7	The Challenge of Poverty in Twenty-First-Century America	103
Notes		117
References		131
Index		147
About the Author		155

Introduction

This book seeks to explore some of the issues that are central to the conversations around diversity and multicultural education. In a work that documented some of the earliest research and explorations on diversity and multicultural education, Banks (2005) articulated multicultural education as an idea, a process, and a reform movement. According to him, multicultural education as an idea holds that all students—regardless of their gender, their social class, or their ethnic, racial, or cultural characteristics—should have an equal opportunity to learn. In this definition of multicultural education, Banks highlighted some of the important themes and issues that must take a center stage in any conversation on diversity and multicultural education: gender, social class, and ethnic, racial, or cultural characteristics. These issues are only representative of the many issues that must be engaged with for any meaningful discussion of multicultural education to take place.

In this book, therefore, certain issues have been carefully selected as issues that need to be investigated and meaningfully engaged in an attempt to understand equity issues and meaningfully engage in multicultural education. The book begins with a discussion of colonialism and colonial legacies that have shaped cultural relations around the globe. The first chapter explains the impact of colonial legacies in shaping relationships between the Western world and the rest of the world. It engages the concepts of power, racial dominance, white privilege, and cultural responsibility in a global society.

The second chapter goes deeper to explain globalization, the idea of a global community, global citizenship, and its implications and mandates for engagement across cultures. The chapter highlights basic aspects of globalization that must be considered as we engage in multicultural education. The chapter engages the idea of multicultural education in an age of globalization. The chapter examines globalization as a twenty-first-century phenomenon. It examines the ideas of a global community, global citizenship, and their implications for multicultural education.

The third chapter discusses the Federal Affirmative Action program, which is aimed at making right decades of wrongs done to ethnic minorities in the United States through racist laws and institutional discrimination. The chapter explores the history of affirmative action, the challenges the law has faced since its inception, its current state and impact on the US educational and social landscape, examples from other parts of the world, as well as the implications it bears for equal educational opportunities in the twenty-first century.

The fourth chapter explores gender issues at the global level. Starting with a discussion of the various ways in which women's rights have been restricted in many parts of the world, the chapter highlights various struggles for women's rights in Africa, the Middle East, and other parts of the world. It discusses global initiatives that have shaped the struggle for women's rights as well as led to advancements in women's rights at a global level. The chapter concludes by highlighting areas where the struggle for gender equity continues into the twenty-first century.

The fifth chapter explores the struggle for women's rights and gender equity in the United States, highlighting the various issues that have limited women's rights in the United States, beginning from the colonial days. The chapter highlights the many US movements and laws that have advanced women's rights. It also highlights prominent women whose roles in the US public arena have promoted women's rights as well as advanced the course of humanity at large.

The sixth chapter focuses on the topic of religious diversity and the battle for religious rights in the United States educational setting. Beginning with a discussion of the US constitutional provisions for religious freedom, the chapter engages the issue of freedom of religion as a constitutional right of all Americans. Various laws and lawsuits that have often challenged this freedom are discussed, and their impacts on the place of religion in the American schools are highlighted. The place of Islam in the US educational setting is discussed extensively.

The last chapter engages a discussion of the problem of poverty as it impacts education in the United States and the world at large. World poverty is briefly discussed, then a more in-depth look on poverty in the United States is undertaken, with the goal of highlighting the history and forms of poverty in the United States as well as some government actions at addressing the problem of poverty.

The topics discussed in this book do not provide for an exhaustive listing of the issues that need to be addressed in a meaningful engagement with multicultural education. Such issues as social welfare, gender identity, and sexual orientation are all topics that still need to be addressed. The scope of this work is limited, but the author will continue to produce more work that will address some of the other issues that have been omitted in this book.

Chapter One

From Colonialism to a Global Community

CHAPTER OBJECTIVES

The goal of this chapter is to engage the concept of global community as a by-product of the combined forces of colonialism and globalization. Utilizing insights from the history of Western colonial activities of the past, this chapter confronts actions that have led to some of the contemporary challenges of today's global societies. With an in-depth discussion of the concepts of globalization, white privilege, and cultural humility, this chapter provides insights into the forces that have shaped the contemporary multicultural societies of the world, and the accompanying globalization trends.

INTRODUCTION

The United Nations Charter opened with the following declaration:

We the peoples of the United Nations determined

- to save succeeding generations from the scourge of war, which twice in our lifetime has brought untold sorrow to mankind, and
- to reaffirm faith in fundamental human rights, in the dignity and worth of the human person, in the equal rights of men and women and of nations large and small, and
- to establish conditions under which justice and respect for the obligations arising from treaties and other sources of international law can be maintained, and
- to promote social progress and better standards of life in larger freedom.

The discipline of multicultural education has focused on the reaffirmation of faith in the fundamental rights of all humans, and in the dignity and worth of every person, regardless of ethnicity, race, gender, socioeconomic status, or sexual orientation. As an academic discipline, it has confronted the academy with the challenge of reframing old and archaic constructs around race, ethnicity, gender, and sexual orientation. This is among the desired goals of multicultural education in the K–12 setting.

As a matter of praxis, however, the academy continues to struggle with what Ali Mazrui (1990) has described as "obstinate dichotomy," in which people are seen in a "persistent conceptualization" of the world as "us versus them," "friend versus foe," and I would add "alien versus native." This perspective, if restricted to the zone of dualism as a matter of conceptualization and academic dialogue, would not pose as much threat, but given the historical baggage of racism, bigotry, and ethnocentrism that has characterized it in the West, it remains a lethal threat to the actualization of lofty goals like the ones expressed in the preamble of the United Nations Charter.

While many Western peoples, especially those in the academy, have a genuine desire to move things along in the direction of humans rights and the affirmation of the worth of all persons, the underlying dualism that says we are different and therefore essentially incongruent, continues to besiege every attempt at healthy integration, or what contemporary leaders of the diversity movement have termed Inclusive Excellence.

In this chapter, we will present a cursory overview of the ways in which colonial ideologies have shaped the contemporary Western worldviews with a strong slant toward white privilege and superiority as a major deterrent to a meaningful engagement with inclusivity. We will confront the idea of white privilege and counterbalance it with the idea of cultural responsibility and cultural humility. Then we will discuss the emergence of world systems and globalization as forces that make inclusivity an inescapable reality for a healthy society.

COLONIALISM, POWER, AND DOMINANCE IN THE NINETEENTH AND TWENTIETH CENTURIES

The nineteenth and early twentieth centuries marked the era of an unbridled spread of European power and dominance across the globe. Between 1884 and 1885, prominent European nations met in a conference room in Berlin and partitioned the continent of Africa among themselves. Western European contact with Africa that started in the fifteenth century as trade missions turned into a mission of conquest and dominance. Nations like Portugal, which had maintained a respectful trade relationship with African kingdoms like the Benin Empire in southwestern Nigeria, morphed into conquerors and colonial masters of African peoples.[1]

The domination of Africa by Europe did not go down without intense resistance. A writer states that "Africans did not lightly lay down their independence . . . the 1890s was a period of widespread African resistance to European conquest."[2] Shillington (2012) remarked that, "In earlier centuries African rulers had generally been able to hold their own against invading European armies. They built up their own arsenal of muzzle-loading guns and made skillful use of more traditional weapons and guerrilla tactics. In the 1870s, however, African armies were rapidly overtaken by advances in European weaponry."[3]

The relevance of the direct quote above focuses on the concept of racial superiority, which developed along with the growth of transatlantic slave trade and the colonization of Africa. As Western Europeans conquered lands and seas through the advancement of their weapons of warfare, they began to assign their success to more than military might. They began to articulate a concept of racial superiority, which not only gave them the right to conquer foreign lands, but to enslave their peoples. These concepts of racial superiority, which did not exist in the earlier encounters, have, sadly, undergirded the way Western Europe has related to the rest of the non-Western world since colonialization.

POWER, DOMINANCE, AND CULTURAL VALUES IN COLONIAL ENCOUNTERS

Conflicting worldviews and value systems characterized the encounters between Europeans and non-European peoples, especially between Africans and Europeans. While Europeans seem to see the world from a worldview shaped by scarcity of resources that necessitated competition and conquest, the African worldview is anchored on the concept of plenty and sufficiency, which stems from a desire for coexistence and cooperation.

The concept of *Ubuntu* is a Southern African concept that anchors human relationships on kindness and the affirmation of the humanity of all, and an understanding of a universal bond between all humanity. The concept of *Ubuntu* assumes that harm done to you is harm done to me. It espouses the codependency of human life and coexistence.

The Igbos of Southeastern Nigeria, distant relatives of South African Bantu tribes, share this very concept. The Igbo have a maxim that says *"Egbe bere ugo bere"* ("Let the hawk perch, and let the eagle perch as well"). The idea here is that there is room for all. This means that your existence or presence does not threaten mine. There is room enough for both of us.

The Africans did not feel threatened by the inroads of Europeans into African lands. They welcomed the Europeans in many cases, until the Europeans began to work against the African interests. Even after the European attitudes changed, the Africans never gave up on their kindness and their hospitality to strangers. This is why, even after years of colonialism and Western abuse, Africans still welcome strangers with open hands. They believe that the world is large enough for all of us. This spirit of coexistence seems distant in many European worldviews.

POWER AND RACIAL DOMINANCE IN THE UNITED STATES AS COLONIAL LEGACIES

One would be right to question the relevance of this argument in twenty-first-century post-colonial America and in the discourse of cultural diversity in the United States and the world. The relevance lies in the idea of colonial legacies and its impact on Western worldviews. Beyond colonization, the Western world, whether they were active or passive participants in the nineteenth- and twentieth-century colonization programs, have engaged with the rest of the word in what De L'Estoile (2008) has termed "colonial relations."

De L'Estoile draws a distinction between colonial relations and colonization, stating that while colonization is the political control of a foreign territory with the goal of exploitation and incorporation into the powers of the colonizing nation, colonial relations speaks to the various ways in which western Europe has generally interacted with the rest of the world between the eighteenth and the twentieth centuries. The nature of these relations has included conquest, repression, religious conversion, scientific exploration, educational and medical missions, trade and commerce, exploitation of the arts, economy, and even the population.

These interactions have left behind colonial legacies that have lasted into the twenty-first century. De L'Estoile argued that all peoples of European descent have participated in the colonial experience whether they directly or indirectly participated in colonization. As such, they have been gifted with legacies, or what one would call cultural scripts, on how to relate to the rest of the world. Wale and Foster (2007) put it this way: "During the period of colonial expansion, various forms of travelers' tales, racial taxonomies, and 'race science' functioned to constitute the discourse that legitimized many institutional forms of racist domination including slavery, colonialism, segregation and apartheid."[4]

COLONIAL LEGACIES AND THEIR IMPACTS ON THE UNITED STATES' WORLDVIEWS

In the United States, British colonialists, spurred by a sense of ethnic and religious superiority, were intent on creating a homogenous society. Other Europeans were expected to assimilate and be absorbed into a dominant Anglo culture. The idea of nativism developed quite early in the American experience, and it created a wedge toward a meaningful integration of others who looked different or spoke in a different language.

So, when the legacy of slavery, Indian displacement, colonial relations, and xenophobia intersected in the US context, a society was created that has struggled for decades to reconcile the promise of unity in her Bill of Rights and an entrenched worldview of a dichotomous world. The call of multiculturalism or inclusive excellence is for a world of cross-cultural affirmation, cultural and social integration, to the point that the humanity of all people is affirmed and their opportunities in the world fostered.

For a Western person to engage this task, he/she must first confront the colonial legacies that have been handed down, confront the dualistic worldview that has shaped their societies, deal with it, and overcome it. To deal with these issues, one must first confront the idea of white racial identity, white privilege, and cultural responsibility.

White Racial Identity Issues

White racial consciousness and white racial identity have anchored on white consciousness and awareness of clearly defined boundaries between groups of people. These boundaries are often determined by ethnic and cultural distinctions around skin color, language, religion, and country of origin.[5]

White racial consciousness can be put simply as the consciousness of being primarily white as a distinguishing factor that separates someone from non-white people. It speaks to the benefits and significances of whiteness compared with those who are outside of that designation.[6] It was Janet E. Helms who in 1984 first pointed out the significance of white racial attitudes in the formation of white racial identity.

A common assumption that underlies white racial identity development in research has been identified by Ellis (2002), and Sue (1981) as follows:

- Racism is seen as an integral part of the American society, and it is seen as permeating every part of the American culture and institutions.

- White people are socialized into the American culture, and they intentionally or unintentionally take the biases, stereotypes, and racist beliefs, attitudes, and behaviors that are part of the American society.
- White people develop a racial consciousness and identity that progresses from oblivion to differences in race and ethnicity to an identity that is affirming of the white superiority consciousness.

Racial and ethnic identity development, according to Helms (1990) and Phinney (1990), anchors on a positive appraisal of one's group, knowledge of and interest in that group, and purposeful engagement with the activities or traditions of that group.

The significance of an understanding of white racial consciousness and white racial identity lies in the fact that individuals who are of the white hue need to confront the fact that through a process of enculturation, they have been predisposed to look at the world through a certain pair of lenses that tend to thrive on ensuring racial boundaries as protective barriers for the safety of the white race to the exclusion of other races of humans. Whether or not one is conscious of these barriers is not the problem in question; rather, what needs to be confronted is that this is a lived experience that must be critically engaged before we can begin to experience healthy cross-cultural relationships in the world.

White Privilege versus Cultural Responsibility

The idea of white privilege builds on the notion that whites accrue certain unique privileges by simply being white. These privileges have supposedly been secured through the combined forces of domination, acts, decisions, and policies that have advantaged whites over other ethnic groups in the society.[7] Hossain (2015) defined white privilege as unearned advantages that people of white skin color enjoy consciously or unconsciously. Tim Wise (2014) described white privilege as advantages, opportunities, benefits, head starts, and/or protections that one receives as white, which may not be available to non-whites.

James Scheurich (1998) paints an image of white privilege as someone walking down the street and having money put into his/her pocket without the individual's knowledge. Leonardo (2004) posits a contrast to this perspective in relation to the experience of ethnic minority people as someone walking down the street and having money removed from the person's pocket.

In a 1988 paper, Peggy McIntosh articulated about fifty elements that would constitute white privilege. Among these were such things as shopping alone and being pretty sure you are not going to be followed along or harassed by a store employee; never being asked to speak for all the people in your race; and having no problem finding housing in a neighborhood where people approve of your household. Economic privilege is a very powerful dynamic, yet many who enjoy it deny that it exists.

South Africa presents a classic case of white privilege combined with economic privilege. For generations, the whites in South Africa had total control of the economic, political, and social infrastructure of the society, dehumanizing the blacks and denying them access to any of these resources through the policy of apartheid. While the end of apartheid has brought the blacks into the political powerhouse of South African government, the whites have kept all the inherited assets of apartheid, and the blacks remain marginalized in the economic landscape of the society.[8] Many South Africans believe that with the end of apartheid there is need for the redistribution of South Africa's natural resources, especially land, which has remained in the hands of white South Africans. Just recently, Donald Trump was trumping up white racial prejudice in tweeting that South Africans are killing white farmers and taking their land. He has never expressed any regard for centuries of injustice that whites have meted out on blacks, beginning with slavery in Europe and the Americas, to apartheid in South Africa.

Dunlap, Scoggin, Green, and Davi (2007) defined the economically privileged as those who were reared in markedly more stable financial and socioeconomic conditions than individuals whom they serve or work with. According to Dunlap et al. (2007), the awareness of privilege leads to such feelings as divided self and cognitive dissonance. They argue that it is important for whites to develop a positive and/or healthy sense of white racial self, which accepts the socialized implications of being white, and for them to develop a sense of themselves as racialized human beings and not to rely on the assumed superiority of whites over other peoples.

UNDERSTANDING THE NEXUS OF PRIVILEGE

The nexus of white privilege is characterized by multiple factors such as access, finance, safety, housing, opportunities, and acceptability (see Figure 1.1). Let's examine each of these factors.

Access

White privilege speaks to the ability of a white individual to enter any office and be respectfully treated by the receptionist, and granted the desired audience regardless of qualifications and social connections. It also speaks to the

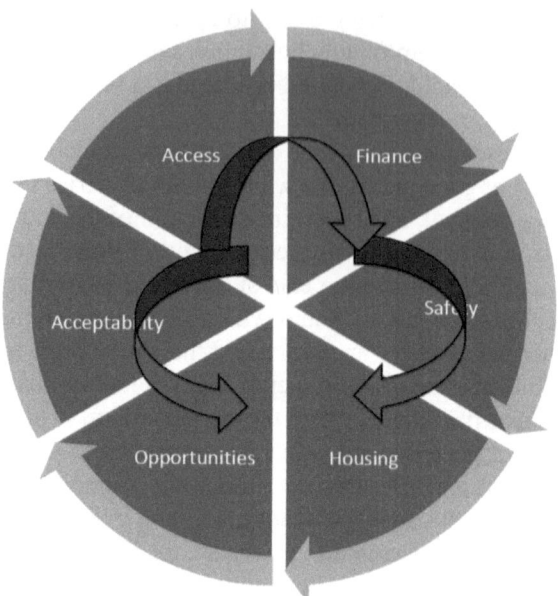

Figure 1.1. Nexus of Privilege

possession of the social networks through family and professional ties; the ability to pick up the phone and call someone in power when help is needed.

Acceptability

Acceptability speaks to the ability to enter into any public and or business space and be accepted as a worthy customer. It means walking through a department store without a store employee walking around to keep their eyes on you. It means choosing to stay late at a public park or to take a late-night stroll in your suburban neighborhood without someone calling the cops to check you out.

Opportunities

Opportunities speak to open doors in career and business, including the ability to seek and secure loans for a mortgage or business, and the ability to secure employment easily and readily in most cases.

Housing

This speaks to your ability to choose where to live, to go out and secure a place there without stress or rejection. It is the certainty that even in the twenty-first century, a realtor will not attempt to redirect you to a poorer neighborhood because of your ethnicity.

Safety

This speaks to your ability to go anywhere you want, any time you want to, without fear of police or white supremacists. It speaks to your ability to question the police when stopped and to demand an explanation as to why you were stopped without getting into more trouble.

White Privilege as a By-Product of Colonialism and Colonial Relations

White privilege is undeniably a logical by-product of the combined forces of colonialism, domination, and colonial relations. Having already explained what we mean by colonialism and colonial relations, let's look at domination. The idea of domination manifests itself in the Western practice of having the white race as the representative of the human race, while the rest of the human race is described or defined in subcategories.

Even in the twenty-first century, the American journalist and newscaster is comfortable describing a white man who was involved in crime as "a man" but makes sure to describe the other person as "a black man," confident that just calling the white person a man is clear enough to everyone, while the other man needs an ethnic categorization to distinguish him from the rest of men. This way of thinking, according to Leonardo (2004), projects the white supremacist, the patriarchal, and capitalist white person as the standard human, while the rest of the humans are fragments.

Ta-Nehisi Coates, in his book, *Between the World and Me* (2015), makes the point that this way of thinking meant that blacks, whether rich or poor, were seen as "less than" the white man. This way of thinking is not only found in the economic and political arenas of America's interactions with the world, they are found in the centuries of Western Christian mission that has impacted the world in different ways.

Western invasion of the non-Western world involved a three-prong approach of trade, colonization, and Christianization. While traders exchanged cheap Western guns, umbrellas, and toilet soap with Africa for her gold, silver, copper, diamond, and many other minerals, the colonial rulers subjugated the people in their own land into slavery, often making them carry them on stretchers and sometimes on their shoulders as their mode of transportation.

The missionaries, in their own activities, destabilized societies with a reckless dismissal and devastation of everything indigenous in terms of worldview and religious expression, and replaced them with Western religious worldviews that are often far removed from authentic biblical worldviews. Africans were required to take on Western names like Dominic, Ferdinand, and Kinsley as evidence of Christianization. Even twenty-first-century long-term and short-term missions, which are often carried out by Christian colleges and universities in the United States, continue to perpetuate the same racial superiority that has been the *modus operandi* of Western contacts with the non-Western world.

The relevance of this argument anchors on the fact that many men and women who work in education, especially in higher education, come from a place of white privilege. Many were born and raised in white communities, attended all-white schools (whether public or private), were taught by teachers who looked like them, and grew up believing that what they and their parents had was the end product of personal rigor and hard work. These men and women grew up often unaware of the institutional structures that enabled them and their parents to earn what they had, while at the same time making it difficult and often impossible for those from ethnic minority groups to earn equally, no matter how hard they tried.

According to Leonardo (2004), while it is a fact that today's whites did not participate in slavery (and colonialization), they have continued to re-create white supremacy on a daily basis. He argues that they perpetuate white supremacy through "color-blindness, ahistorical justification, and sleights-of-mind."[9] White privilege is a place of comfort and convenience, and those who enjoy it may not want to critique it lest they begin to feel guilty about it. Many of those who enjoy white privilege have accepted the social narrative that the minority are lazy, foolish, and morally lax; that's why they are suffering.

Granted such an excuse, it would not make sense to self-reflect on the imbalance of economic and other opportunities in society. Most marginalized groups in white privileged societies are coming from decades, if not centuries, of damage to the human spirit, which has resulted in all kinds of social ills: violence, mental problems, inferiority complexes, poor health, and many other ills.[10] This would be the case with the United States of America (Native Americans and African Americans), as well as with South Africa.

An awareness, therefore, of the influences of colonialism, colonial relations, domination, and white privilege calls for the practitioner in the American educational context to begin to engage the world outside of his/her comfort level. Incidentally, the forces of globalization and America's history as a nation of immigrants have made it certain that you do not need to leave your town or city to experience diversity. Diversity is coming to every nook and corner of America's towns and villages and the world at large.

Many educators, however, still think they can work and operate effectively without engaging the diversity around them. Survival in the twenty-first-century academic context calls for cultural and intercultural competency. These goals are not attainable without cultural humility. So, let's first engage the idea of cultural humility and its value in the educational setting.

THE IDEA OF CULTURAL HUMILITY

Trevalon and Murray-Gaercia (1998) have been credited with introducing the concept of cultural humility in the practice of social work, and the concept has been adopted and used in various forms in both social work and clinical psychology.[11] Westerners, and especially Westerners in higher education, come from a place of privilege and power shaped by entrenched social imbalance that was influenced by concepts of race, power, and privilege that have often produced negative impacts of racism, injustice, discrimination, and repression upon the minority populations.

For some decades now, voices in the multicultural education movement have called for those who work in contexts that require them to interface with people from ethnic minority groups, such as social workers, clinical psychologists, and educators, to be equipped with cultural competency skills. Ortega and Faller (2011) identified the essential elements of cultural competency to include: a) valuing diversity, b) developing cultural self-awareness, c) appreciating the dynamics of cross-cultural interactions, d) being knowledgeable about within-group cultural differences, and e) the ability to deliver relevant and responsive services to the diverse and complex needs of individuals, families, social networks, and communities.[12]

Fisher-Borne, Cain, and Martin (2015) contend that many cultural competency models tend to focus on creating a comfortable environment for the Western practitioners as opposed to making them self-aware of the power differentials that exist between them and other people. Some of these cultural competency models, they argue, fail to account for the complex history and reality of inequalities that exist across the areas of health, economic, and social issues and concerns.

Bennett[13] developed what he called the Developmental Model of Intercultural Sensitivity (DMIS), arguing that the development of intercultural competency happens in developmental stages. According to him, individuals often start by experiencing their own culture as the only real culture, with other cultures either not understood or dismissed with a simplistic excuse. (This is called Denial of Differences.)

Bennett states that individuals progress from this stage to a stage of defense against differences, and from there they move to a stage of minimization of differences, to acceptance of differences, adaptation to differences, and on to integration of differences, in which a person's experience of the self is expanded to include the ability to shift from one cultural worldview to another (Intercultural Development Research [IDR] Institute, 2014). Fisher-Borne, Cain, and Martin (2015) articulated this shift as a movement from ethnocentric to ethno-relative worldviews, describing an ethno-relative worldview as the ability to perceive self as "situated in a world with myriad of legitimate cultural differences."[14]

The idea of cultural humility, on the other hand, is defined by Tervalon and Murray-Garcia (1998) as incorporating a lifelong commitment to self-evaluation, critique, redress of power imbalance, and the development of mutually beneficial and non-paternalistic partnerships with the individuals, communities, and defined populations with whom we interact. Cultural humility is multidimensional, comprised of a willingness to accurately appraise the self, an orientation toward others, the ability to regulate one's emotions, interpersonal receptivity, and an appreciation of the value in things.[15]

Ortega and Faller (2011), on the other hand, presented cultural humility as having three dimensions:

- Promotion of self-awareness: This means that people are able to accept and appreciate their unique cultural perspective, and how that shapes the lenses from which they view the world and reality.
- Openness: This implies that the individual is able to appreciate the fact that he/she does not and cannot know all there is to know about the world and the persons with whom he/she interacts on a daily basis.
- Transcendence: This means that the individual understands and accepts his place and role in the world as very small when placed in the larger context of the world and reality.[16]

Cultural competency and cultural humility, while similar in their goals, have essential differences that set them apart. Cultural competence assumes the problem of lack of knowledge, awareness, and skills in individuals and organizations, seeking to develop knowledge, skills, and values that would enable them to work across lines of differences. Cultural humility assumes the need to understand the self, the others, communities, and colleagues, with humility; a recognition of the imbalance of power, and the goal of challenging the imbalance, ensuring institutional accountability, and ongoing critical self-reflection.[17]

So, the idea of cultural humility in our culturally diverse society suggests that one accepts the reality of his/her ethnocentric worldviews, accepts the inadequacy of his/her worldviews to fully make meaning of the world, and appreciates, engages with, and seeks out ways to tap into the resources outside of his/her cultural experiences to better understand the world and the people he/she interacts with on a daily basis, who may be different from him/her.

Cultural humility leads to a less deterministic and less authoritative understanding of the world and its cultures and peoples. Certain skills are considered essential to cultural humility, among which are a) active listening, b) reflecting (or reflective listening), c) reserving judgment, and d) entering the other's world (making efforts to see the world from the worldview of the other person).[18] Ortega and Faller (2011) tend to see cultural competency and cultural humility as different but related concepts, but they assume that cultural competence is impossible without cultural humility. Cultural humility, though a developmental process, when carefully and consistently pursued, leads not just to cultural competence, but to intercultural competence.

Granted the enduring legacy of colonial influences in shaping the worldview among white Americans, it means that any meaningful engagement with multiculturalism that seeks to produce long-lasting effects on individuals and institutional structures must begin with the development of cultural humility. It is impossible to engage the "other" in a healthy and affirming way as long as we see them as "less than." Cultural humility accepts that mine is just one of the many cultures there are. It accepts that while my worldview may be rich and pragmatic, other peoples' worldviews are equally rich and pragmatic, and I will see the richness and pragmatism of those worldviews if I can engage with them and be open to learning from them.

This openness to "the other" is no longer an optional disposition in the twenty-first century. During the nineteenth and twentieth centuries, the world remained separate and apart as communication modalities and transportation apparatuses remained slow and difficult. The twenty-first century and the dawn of the new age of the information superhighway has narrowed the distance between our worlds, and humanity has been drawn closer to one another in an unprecedented way. In the subsequent section, we will engage the emergence of the world systems and the globalization tendencies that have set this age apart from the previous ones.

THE EMERGENCE OF WORLD SYSTEMS AND GLOBALIZATION

World Systems Theory has been described as an attempt to make sense of the political, economic, and social histories of the modern societies.[19] Tracing World Systems Theory to a product of Marxist intellectual revival, Shannon

(1992) explains that World Systems Theory rejects the structural-functional theory of modernization, which assumes that every society is capable of emerging from kinship systems to contemporary modernized societies. Modernization theory believes that all societies go through certain phases at one point or the other, and that they eventually evolve into modern states similar to what you see in Western Europe and North America.

World Systems Theory, however, assumes a structure in which the relationships among societies consist of a coherent fixed pattern. This pattern is described as composed of a hegemonic core and an exploited periphery (see Figure 1.2). This describes the relationship that has existed between the Western European nations and the rest of the world since the beginning of the Western exploration and colonization. The core nations were the centers of production, while the periphery nations served as the sources of the raw material and the market for the finished goods.

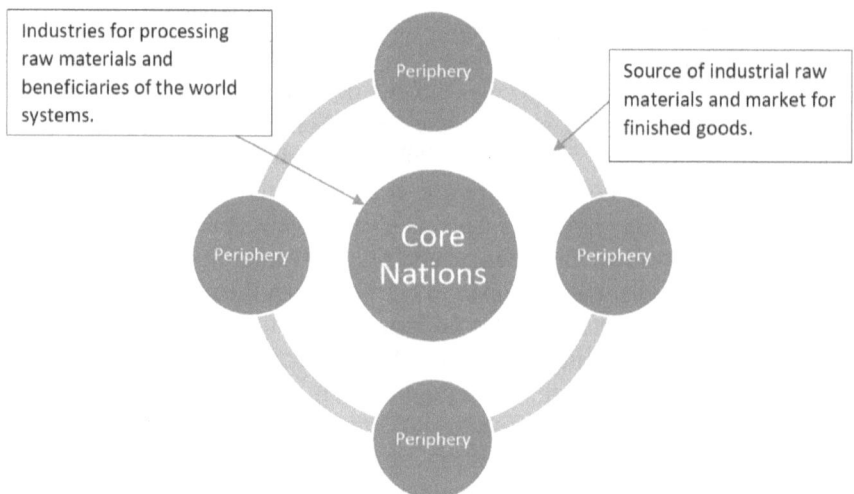

Figure 1.2. World Systems

This was a system that had been largely controlled by Western European powers and the United States going into the twenty-first century. It was a system that fostered what Komlosy, Boatca, and Notle (2016) described as "inequalities of race, ethnicity, gender, epistemic status, and economic position put in place during colonial rule,"[20] and these have largely translated into enduring inequalities that have lasted into the postcolonial eras.

The flaw of the World Systems Theory is that development was narrowly defined within economic confines and probably within the limited confines of Western educational structures and schemes. This narrow definition of development is what gave Western Europeans the moral impetus to destroy and displace many non-Western societies in the name of civilization and development. Empires and peoples with highly developed cultures and educational structures that preceded Western civilization were destroyed in Africa and other parts of the world.

There was a reckless disregard of the cultures and worldviews of other people as westernization programs that aimed at nothing but fast-tracking the extraction and removal of indigenous resources was pursued by Western powers. Western powers produced and propagated dominant ideologies that narrowly defined development within Western frames of reference, producing a Western hegemony that has been reproduced and perpetuated over the centuries through Western institutions and structures, whether in Europe and America, or in the rest of the world.

The end result of this is that even in the twenty-first century, Euro-American frames of reference have remained the vehicle for framing the idea of development. This bifurcation grounded in White Supremacy is referred to by Ali Mazrui as Global Apartheid. This is a world in which the whites exercise supreme control over power (political and social) and economic resources. South African former president Thabo Mbeki used this phrase in 2001 to describe Africa's economic experience over the past fifty years.[21] With the emergence of what Dunaway and Cleland (2016) have termed semi-periphery nations such as India and China, nations that are currently preying on less developed nations for their natural resources, the idea of the dominance of Western (or Euro-American) hegemony is currently being challenged as the prevailing force at play.

Oliverio and Lauderdale (2016) argued to depart from looking at the world relations in terms of world systems, but to see it as a "World System." They see a World System that has been in existence over five thousand years, in which imperialism and coercion have dominated the world with the locus of power shifting between the East and the West. They quote Andre Gunder Frank (1998), who called the rise of Western societies a blip in what was otherwise an Asian-centered economy.

The problem with this view is captured in an observation by Komlosy, Boatca, and Notle (2016), that while the twenty-first century has been characterized by a declining hegemony of any one nation or bloc of nations, the polarizations and global inequalities have continued. The twenty-first century is marked by a major convergence of world powers socially, politically, and economically into what we have popularly termed *globalization*. Yet many non-Western nations continue to suffer.

Chase-Dunn (2013) identified five linked crises that are simultaneously occurring to shape the twenty-first century. These are listed as:

- Crises of hegemony and global governance;
- Crises of inequality and democracy;
- Crisis in the relationship between humans and the natural environment;
- Crises in the global capitalist system; and
- Crises in the New Global Left.[22]

Andre Frank (1998) described this world system as characterized by center versus periphery structure, hegemony versus rivalry competition, and cyclical ups and downs. Fueled by breakthroughs in communication and transportation, globalization has introduced a new dynamic into the world marketplace, namely, accelerated transnational migration. As a result of globalization, the world is coming together into an intricate network of shared interests and unavoidable responsibilities.

While the nineteenth and twentieth centuries were marked by unrestricted movement of Western Europeans and Americans to the ends of the earth in pursuit of trade and other interests for their own social mobility, the world is coming to America and Europe in the twenty-first century. These transnational migrations present a form of social mobility for nations that used to be at the periphery.

World Systems scholarship asserts that migration to more wealthy regions of the world is the most effective means toward social mobility for populations at the periphery. This means that transnational migration is something the West must be prepared to live with in a world where distance has narrowed, and communication has become less restricted.[23]

The sociopolitical outcomes of globalization in Western societies are readily observable in the growing diversity that is visible in many European nations and in the United States. As the world comes to the West, they bring with them their languages, worldviews, and cultural practices. The homogeneity that Western European nations enjoyed is quickly disappearing, and the cultural hegemony that had previously characterized America as a dualism of white and colored people is also being challenged.

Peoples from Asian nations want to be known as Koreans, Japanese, Thai, and so on, not as Asians. African peoples want to be known as Nigerians, Ghanaians, Ethiopians, and so on, not as blacks or simply Africans. This evokes what Dunway and Clelland (2016) termed "the troubled relationship between the white European world and the world of those defined by whites as 'dark others.'"[24]

The age-long categorizations of whites and non-whites, superior and inferior, is being challenged at all levels. This has resulted in what Robinson (2016) has described as "reactionary politics, xenophobia and discrimination against 'foreign aliens,'" which is evident in the recent action of British citizens to break with the European Union (Brexit), and the rise of Donald Trump in the United States, who recently ran a presidential campaign representing a racist and nativist movement calling for the removal of immigrants and the building of walls to ward off the world. When these movements call for a return to the past, they are asking for a return to a system that fostered inequalities of race, ethnicity, gender, epistemic status, and economic conditions that characterized the era of colonialism.[25]

Under the colonial frame of reference, the epistemic status of the non-Westerner was regarded as inferior and subordinate to the whites. These views were perpetuated in schools, colleges, and universities in Europe and the United States. As the world continues to converge, however, faculty at these schools, colleges, and universities are coming in contact with their non-Western faculty colleagues, who are not their inferior by any measure.

Many of these schools, colleges, and universities have, however, continued to struggle with how to bring these "other people" into the fold as faculty and administrators on equal standing. Christian colleges and universities, who carry with them both colonial and missionary worldviews in how they see the world, are actually much less progressive in their interactions with other non-Western colleagues than the secular institutions.

Chapter Two

Globalization and Multiculturalism

CHAPTER OBJECTIVES

The goal of this chapter is an in-depth discussion of the concepts and ideas of globalization, global community, global citizenship, and the implications they bear for multicultural education in the twenty-first century. Immigration, transportation, and communication will be discussed as areas in which globalization has manifested itself at the world stage. The implications these bear for educational curriculum and practices will also be discussed.

GLOBALIZATION AND MULTICULTURALISM AS PHENOMENA OF THE TWENTY-FIRST CENTURY

Globalization can be defined as the convergence of the economic, social, and political forces of the world in such a way that a strong tread of interdependency is woven through world societies to the extent that individual and group lives and existence become codependent upon those of others outside of the self and nation states. Since the 1990s, we have seen a wave of expectations and hopes of a new dawn in human history when our sense of self and nationhood will become inextricably tied to those of others in such a way that we are able to forge ahead into a new World Order of harmonious and peaceful coexistence.

World leaders, from Mikhail Gorbachev in 1988 to Barack Obama in 2010, alluded to and desired for a one world order of peace and harmonious existence. Obama talked about a new world order "that's based on a different set of principles, that's based on a sense of common humanity, that's based on economies that work for all people."[1] Globalization as an idea, therefore, presents the promise of utopia when looked at from a theoretical perspective. The last two decades, however, have seen globalization in real force, and one would concede to the fact that while it has not ushered the world into a utopia, life in society has changed significantly in every nation on Planet Earth.

While the 1970s and 1980s launched the United States and a few other Western nations into the arena of multiculturalism and a critical engagement with how to live life in a diverse society, the 2000s have ushered the world into globalization and the challenge of living life not just as individuals and groups within one nation-state, but as global citizens, whose reach extend beyond national boundaries. When social scientists have studied globalization, they have seen it mostly as visible within a pattern of exchange of goods, people, information, and services across independent and autonomous nation states.[2]

Many researchers have not paid much attention to culture and multiculturalism within the context of the study of globalization. Some who have paid attention to it have made a quick stopover at culture's door by acknowledging certain cultural implications of globalization. Some, however, have engaged the intersections of culture and globalization in depth, and one such study is by Robert Lieber and Ruth Weisberg (2002), who saw culture as the primary carrier of globalization, and the accompanying modern values, and also as constituting the arena within which national, religious, and ethnic identities are contested in a global society.

According to these researchers, culture constitutes the arena within which the most fundamental questions of human identities of ethnic, religious, social, personal, and national identity are confronted. Cultural identity has been traditionally shaped around ethnicity, religion, country of origin, and such. With globalization, we meet a world where national boundaries have become porous in the face of mass immigration, and the idea of global citizenship now stands in direct opposition to ethnic identities. We meet a world where ethnic and religious exclusivity, and social exclusivity, are confronted by a growing convergence of forces that make inclusivity an inescapable demand for life in the twenty-first century. The result has been both positive and negative.

The positive outcomes of globalization are evident in the way people move around today (immigration), the means by which people move around (transportation), and how people speak and interact with one another (communication), as well as the movement of goods and services across national boundaries (commerce). Its negative effects are also evident in the many occurrences of the twenty-first century, beginning with the attack on the US World Trade Center on September 11, 2001, by Muslim fundamentalists who declared war on Western culture and its influences across the globe.

This resistance to globalization has been evidenced in the astronomical growth of terrorist groups like Al-Qaeda, the Islamic State of Iraq and Syria (ISIS), and other such groups. In the West, the resistance is evident in the nativist and Alt Right movements in Europe and the United States. Nativists in Great Britain successfully got the country to vote to leave the European Union in order to stem the flow of immigration and other international social and economic forces into Great Britain. Donald Trump was propelled into power in the United States in 2017 by an Alt Right movement that was anchored in an anti-immigration and antiglobalization ideology.

So, globalization as a social force is facing major resistance in various parts of the world, yet there is no indication that the tide of globalization will be stunted by these movements. To fully understand why the forces of globalization have become basically unstoppable, we need to look more closely at the various ways globalization has affected life and societies in the twenty-first century.

THE IDEA OF GLOBAL COMMUNITY

There has been a lot of buzz recently on the idea of global citizenship. According to Davy, Davy, and Leisering (2013), in this age of globalization, the concept of global citizenship suggests that all persons, regardless of their place of residence, deserve certain rights. These rights, they point out, are well represented in the economic and social rights laid out by the UN in the 1948 Universal Declaration of Human Rights.

The idea of global citizenship suggests the need for people everywhere to be seen as part of one human community. This idea calls for a disconnect with the old dualistic view of the world as "we" versus "them." It calls for a collective engagement in the preservation of human lives everywhere, the preservation of the global ecosystem, and the facilitation of good governance and social order in every society. Seubert (2014) called this global society a transnational civil society. In a world of global interdependence, it is imperative that citizenship at local, national, or global levels includes meaningful inclusion and full and indefinite membership (cf. Seubert, 2014).

This global community is not made up of homogeneity; rather, it is made up of contrasting heterogeneity, yet bound by one contract, one love, and one covenant. They commit to live together, to feed together, and not to harm one another.

The point has been made already that world leaders, from Mikhail Gorbachev (1988) to Barack Obama, have often alluded to and desired for a one world order. The one world Barack Obama talked about has to have a new world order that was based on a different set of principles from what we currently see in the United Nations charter. It was supposed to be a world based on a sense of common humanity and common economies that work for all people (Cilliza, 2014).

This world of utopia sounds more like the biblical utopia painted by the prophet Isaiah: "*The wolf will live with the lamb, the leopard will lie down with the goat, the calf and the lion and the yearling[a] together; and a little child will lead them. The cow will feed with the bear, their young will lie down together, and the lion will eat straw like the ox. The infant will play near the cobra's den, and the young child will put its hand into the viper's nest. They will neither harm nor destroy on all my holy mountain, for the earth will be filled with the knowledge of the Lord as the waters cover the sea*" (Isaiah 11:6–9 NIV). We all know how elusive utopia is for this earthly existence, yet the desire causes us to strive for a better humanity and a better world than we have today.

Effects of Globalization on Societies and Nations

The forces of globalization have reshaped the twenty-first-century world in several major areas. These include migration, communication, and transportation and commerce. The discussion in this section will focus on migration and communication only.

Migration

Mass migration of people is probably one of the most pronounced problems of the twenty-first century so far. Beginning with movements in search of better economic conditions, to forced movements away from home as a result of war or natural disasters that come with climate change, the movement of people across national boundaries in this age is without precedent. At least 244 million people, or 3.3 percent of the world's population, lived outside their own countries of origin in the year 2015.[3] The rapid pace of movement of people across national boundaries is becoming perplexing to nations whose ways of life have been the most impacted by these movements.

According to the International Organization for Migration, the number of international migrants across the globe reached a height of 244 million people in 2015. Of this number, women made up 48 percent.[4] Germany has been at the center of immigration discourses in the past few years, given that it recently ranked the second most popular destination for migrants worldwide. This is as a result of the government's open arm reception of refugees and immigrants from Muslim nations. Greece, in the midst of its economic and political challenges, has had to deal with mass immigration from Syria and

North Africa, as the Mediterranean has become a popular passage for those fleeing wars and economic hardships in both Africa and the Middle East.

The Gulf States of United Arab Emirates, Qatar, and Kuwait are noted to house the highest number of international migrants worldwide, with the foreign-born population of United Arab Emirates at 88.4 percent of the society, those in Qatar made up 75.7 percent, with those in Kuwait at 73.6 percent of the population.[5] In the United States, of the 320.9 million people living there in 2015, 46.6 million were of foreign birth.[6]

According to IOM's World Migration Report, about one in every five migrants in 2015 lived in the top largest twenty cities of the world. That same year, Germany was the largest recipient of first-time individual asylum claims worldwide. A third of the residents of cities such as Auckland, Sydney, London, and Singapore were foreign-born, while one in four residents of Paris, Frankfurt, and Amsterdam were also foreign-born.[7]

The impacts of migrations as the ripple effect of globalization are noticeable both in the host nations of the immigrants and in their home countries. This impact is more traceable when you look at the flow of money. There is a worldwide pattern of immigrants making money in their host countries and sending it back to relatives in their home countries.

In 2015, the Pew Research Center noted that the amount of money remitted by immigrants to their home countries worldwide was almost $600 billion. The Center noted that migration alters both the demographics and the flow of resources in both host countries and home countries.[8] The combined forces of wars, political instability, and globalization have resulted in a heavy flow of refugees and labor migrants globally. Other forces of globalization such as communication, transportation, and commerce have made migration easier and more widespread.

Communication

A Nigerian immigrant to the United States was studying at a United States university in the early 1970s when his father in-law died in Nigeria. The family in Nigeria was desperate to get in touch with him and his wife, because his wife was the eldest daughter and they needed her input in the funeral decisions, so they sent a telegram. After days of waiting in vain for a response, they went ahead and buried their dead. When the dead man's daughter and her husband finally got the telegram, it was already three weeks after her father had been buried. Telegram was supposed to be the fastest mode of communication in the 1970s.

If that had happened today, while the man was still in the hospital in Nigeria, the family in the United States would have been able to have talked directly with him. They would have been able to talk with his doctors, contribute to decisions on his care, and if death did come, they would have been able to know the moment it happened and play the roles they were expected to play, despite the distance. This is how much communication has changed in the twenty-first century. The combined forces of the cell phone, WhatsApp, Instagram, Facebook, Twitter, and other social media applications have made the difference.

Globalization has been identified as the primary force that is shaping the twenty-first-century world. It has brought about an increasingly integrated world economic system, new information and communication technologies, a new stream of international knowledge networks, and the rise of English as the universal language of the scientific community.[9] Innovations in technology have made communication faster and better. From globalization has emerged a network-centric world.

Fryer (2013) described today's world of work as ubiquitous. It is a network-centric world in which so many devices and tools are connected to people, information, and experiences. People are organically connected through multiple platforms that make it possible for people from across the globe to communicate, join forces, and problem-solve together. Technology has not only changed communication; it has also changed the way learning takes place.

The *NMC Horizon Report* for 2017 listed developments in technology that have changed society and the way learning is delivered and received. Some of these include breakthroughs in learning analytics, adaptive learning technologies, the Internet, wearable technologies, artificial intelligence, augmented and virtual reality, robotics, virtual mobile assistants, among many others.[10]

In the twenty-first century, breakthroughs in technology and communication have led to expanded access to learning at a global level. Students in Africa and Asia are taking classes in US institutions and communicating effectively with professors and peers through technology. A dominant characteristic of the twenty-first-century educational landscape is twenty-four hours a day, seven days a week (24/7) with virtual access to information and resources.

There is an astronomical increase in the ability to create multimedia content and share it with the world. There is increased ability and resources to participate in online social networks to share ideas, collaborate, and learn new things. This trend places a new mandate on the educational structures, to revise the educational curriculum, content, and instructional practices to make them cross-cultural, rather than regional. This will be further addressed later.

The Idea of Global Citizenship

Zurcher (1992) defines citizenship as "the most perfect form of membership in a political community."[11] According to Zurcher, a citizen owes an unqualified allegiance to his or her state. This definition of citizenship that suggests an unqualified allegiance is problematic, unless it concedes the rights of citizens to protest and express dissent on issues of concern. The definition is even more problematic in the face of the convergence of global interests in a world that's intricately interconnected.

To hold unqualified allegiance to one nation when your interests and activities transverse national boundaries would be problematic. The global intersection of interests demands that humans no longer look at the world from an ethnocentric perspective, but rather that they begin to see themselves as beings whose existence and the existence of others outside of their locale are inextricably intertwined. While one would do well to hold allegiance to his/her nation-state, global citizens need to seek the interest of other humans beyond their locale if we are to live in a peaceful and harmonious world.

Global citizenship, therefore, is a new dimension of self-identity in which humans are able to define their personhood beyond ethnic, religious, and national distinctives. They are able to seek harmony with those whose ethnic, religious, and national identities may differ from theirs, because they share a common interest and a common fate.

Until recently, individual identity across regions and nations has been shaped by religious, ethnic, national, and regional distinctives. Globalization has, however, brought about a new way for individuals to see themselves. Given that individuals are no longer restricted to interaction with people and forces within their locality, where that remains the case, almost every locale on Planet Earth is becoming more and more diverse and multicultural.

This means that just as humans want to access and appropriate goods and services wherever they may be found, citizenship responsibility is no longer exclusively national or regional. It becomes global. Given that when Hong Kong coughs, New York catches a cold, whether politically or economically, New Yorkers must no longer see themselves as exclusively New Yorkers, but must seek to foster those forces that would keep both Hong Kong and New York peaceful and harmonious.

Osler and Starkey (2003) use the term *cosmopolitan citizenship*, which they define as an idea of citizenship that focuses on human rights, peace, democracy, and development, and the ability to make a difference at both local and global levels. The United Nations International Implementation Scheme for the Decade identified four key values that must underscore a sustainable development of global citizenship. They are as follows:

- Respect for the dignity and rights of all people across the globe, with a commitment to social and economic justice for all people.

Figure 2.1. Global Citizenship

- Respect for the (human) rights of the future generations, with a commitment to intergenerational responsibility.
- Respect and care for life in all its diversity, including the protection and restoration of earth's ecosystems.
- Respect for cultural diversity and a commitment to building and upholding, a global and local culture of nonviolence, tolerance, and peace.[12]

Global citizenship calls for a commitment to the political and economic success of all humanity, beyond the individual interest and the interest of a few nations. It involves a commitment to get along with people who are different from us socially, politically, economically, and culturally.[13] It's a commitment to help lift those in poverty out of poverty and those in oppressive situations out of oppression.

Bahru and Rogers (2016) see this commitment as employing an ethic of care, which leads one to act out of global concerns and an acknowledgment of global interdependence, to seek peace and the well-being of all humanity. According to these authors, global citizenship means that citizenship can no longer be based exclusively on nation of birth; rather it should embrace a sense of interdependence and interconnectedness of all beings. Global citizenship calls for a new generation of citizens who are committed to solving the world's problems, regardless of the region of concentration.

This includes a commitment to solving the problems of global warming, poverty and disease, water scarcity, human rights abuses, conflicts, and wars. It is on the basis of this reality that the study of multicultural education can no longer be engaged in the twenty-first century without due consideration of globalization and its implications for the education of the new and next generations.

EDUCATIONAL IMPLICATIONS OF GLOBALIZATION

The implications of globalization for the educational setting are multiple and varied. The educational implications include issues and conceptions of culture, cultural competency, cross-cultural interactions, educational curriculum, teaching and learning approaches and practices, citizenship education, and much more. For the sake of brevity, we will narrow our discussion to the issues of cross-cultural competency, cross-cultural curriculum, and cross-cultural instructional and teaching practices.

Cross-Cultural Competency

Whereas literature is filled with discussions of cultural competency, which speaks to the need to understand and effectively function with awareness and respect of the complex cultural variables in one's society, cross-cultural or intercultural competency refers to the ability to function effectively when moving away from one's community to another country or culture. Cross-cultural competency speaks to one's comfort level in traversing cultural boundaries and being able to function effectively in that new context.

Globalization and its dynamics place a new mandate on the educational system to not only produce global citizens who are culturally competent within their localities, but global citizens who are able to transverse national, cultural, religious, and social boundaries and effectively function within those different settings. Cross-cultural competency calls for educating the present and the next generation of citizens on how to maneuver through the maze of global societies with respectful and harmonious interactions with people they come across. This demands a new awareness of the place of culture and culture studies in the contemporary educational setting.

The 1970s saw an explosion of ethnic studies in US universities and colleges as African American Studies, Hispanic Studies, and Asian Studies programs mushroomed across universities and colleges of the United States. These developments were the by-product of the civil rights movement and the educational reforms of the 1960s and early 1970s, which gave rights and opportunities to ethnic- and gender-minority people to pursue educational opportunities without hindrance.

A critical review of these programs across the United States today will reveal that more often than not, students enrolled in these programs are primarily students of the same ethnic group that's being studied. This means that these programs have not served as vehicles for cross-cultural education; rather, they have worked to service the needs of particular ethnic groups who seek to know more about their culture and heritage.

A cross-cultural educational focus will probe the intersections of commerce, politics, and culture across communities, nations, and societies. A cross-cultural educational focus also implies that regional or national educational curriculums would be inadequate to produce global citizens. In globalization, culture must no longer be seen as a side effect; instead it needs to be seen as possessing an intrinsic significance given that it encapsulates within its structure, the fundamental questions of human identity of ethnic, personal, national, and religious identities. It deals with the deep-rooted issues of identity and selfhood in every human society.[14]

The educational curricula of the twenty-first-century world need to be cross-cultural and multicultural, employing the constructs, concepts, ideals, ideas, and even educational materials from the global arena, to the preparation of the new global citizens. Students in the United States, in Qatar, Nigeria, or Shanghai, need to be exposed to the works of Chinua Achebe, Wole Soyinka, Amy Tan, and Vijay Prashad, just as much as they should read the works of Ernest Hemingway, Miguel de Cervantes, and William Shakespeare.

Cross-cultural education is an educational imperative of the twenty-first century, and educational curricula across the nations must change to reflect this reality. This fact exposes the sad and pitiable development in the United States where the Common Core State Standards that were aimed at standardizing learning across the states of the nation have been discarded in many states in favor of narrow and shortsighted local curricula that educate within the narrow confines of local preferences.

Curriculum and Instruction in Global Education

The United Nations' 2030 Agenda for Sustainable Development states as follows:

> *We commit to providing inclusive and equitable quality education at all levels—early childhood, primary, secondary, tertiary, technical and vocational training. All people, irrespective of sex, age, race, ethnicity, and persons with disabilities, migrants, indigenous peoples, children and youth, especially those in vulnerable situations, should have access to life-long learning opportunities*

that help them acquire the knowledge and skills needed to exploit opportunities and to participate fully in society. We will strive to provide children and youth with a nurturing environment for the full realization of their rights and capabilities, helping our countries to reap the demographic dividend including through safe schools and cohesive communities and families.[15]

This declaration encapsulates what should be the focus of education in our globalized societies. First, there is the desire for inclusive and equal quality education at all educational levels. Second, there is the focus on access to education and lifelong learning for all humans irrespective of race, gender, age, ethnicity, and disability. Third, there is the focus on the acquisition of knowledge and skills needed for accessing opportunities and full participation in society. This last point, more than any other, speaks to the issue of curriculum. What are those skills and knowledge that individuals need to access opportunities and participate fully in society?

In a study by Plum (2014), six areas of learning that should constitute the curriculum for education in a global society were identified by the Danish Parliament. These areas include the following: science, language and communication, personal development, culture and expression, social development, and body movement. These consist of knowledge-producing practices and social/civic development curriculum. Educational curriculum in a global society must be a force for the development of useful knowledge and empowerment for social and civic engagement for those who go through the educational system.[16]

In a paper on the implications of globalization on education in Malaysia, Fauzan (2007) identified specific elements that should constitute educational curriculum in a globalized society. He calls for educational curriculum to depart from learning that focuses on memory and strive for a "meaningful, socially responsible, multicultural, holistic, and technological curriculum."[17] He calls for curricula that stimulates creativity, thinking, and caring for individual differences and individual learning styles.

The Partnership for 21st Century Learning provided a framework for what should constitute curricula for the twenty-first-century educational setting (see Figure 2.2). The framework focused on the following:

- Life and career skills.
- Learning and innovation skills made up of critical thinking, communication, collaboration, and creativity (the 4cs).
- Information, media, and technology skills.
- The key subjects of reading, writing, and arithmetic (the 3Rs), as well as twenty-first-century themes of (a) global awareness, (b) financial, economic, business, and entrepreneurial literacy, (c) civic literacy, (d) health literacy, and environmental literacy.

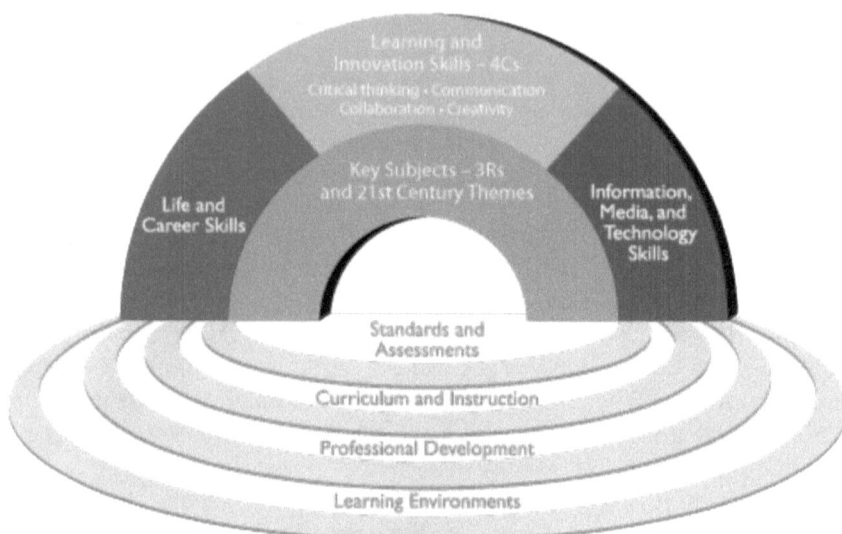

Figure 2.2. Framework for Twenty-First-Century Learning

This framework provides the foundational principles that should guide curriculum development in any society that desires to produce informed global citizens through their educational systems.

In the United States, an effort to align instructional curriculum in the K–12 setting along the demands of the Framework for 21st Century Learning through the Common Core State Standards has hit a major obstacle course. This obstacle course must be overcome in any society that desires to produce global citizens through their educational system. To fully address this obstacle, let's look briefly at the history of the Common Core State Standards in the United States.

HISTORY OF COMMON CORE STATE STANDARDS (CCSS)

In 2007, the National Governors Association (NGA) and the Council of Chief State School Officers (CCSSO) released a report indicating that in order to achieve a world-class education for American students, there needed to be a common benchmark for all students. Two years later, in 2009, governors and state commissioners of education in forty-eight US states launched a movement toward a common national standard. This is the movement that led to the creation of the Common Core State Standards (CCSS). The goal was to develop a uniform and consistent set of standards that would ensure that US students are properly equipped with skills and competencies they need for college and career, upon completion of high school education.

By late 2009, President Barack Obama infused a new vitality into the Common Core Movement through Race to the Top (RttT), a program that aimed at infusing $350 million in grant money into the development of tests that would be aligned to the Common Core State Standards.[18] This led to a four-year grant awarded to two consortiums: the Smarter Balanced Assessment Consortium (SBAC), and the Partnership for Assessment of Readiness for College and Careers (PARCC). Both consortiums aimed at developing an assessment that would focus on problem-solving and the application of knowledge, moving away from multiple choice, factual recall that characterized previous assessments (Jochim & McGuinn, 2016).

In early 2009, the federal government made available $4.35 billion in funding to encourage states to adopt better standards and assessment toward more effective schools.[19] This grant encouraged most states to sign on to the Common Core State Standards. In 2011, just one year after the standards were released, forty-five states and the District of Columbia had adopted both the standards and one of the two versions of the assessments that go with it.[20] By 2012, the US Virgin Islands had joined in the adoption.[21] This was probably the highest number of states that adopted these standards before it began its downward slide.

Once the adoption of Common Core reached the height indicated above, media coverage began to reveal a mixture of perceptions and reception of the new standards and the accompanying assessments. Various factors led to these reactions, among which were implementation challenges, distrust of government and governmental involvement, and distrust of big business and big business involvement. These were just a few of the many factors that raised concerns in various quarters about Common Core.

Pense, Freeburg, and Clemon (2015) described the many voices and positions that engaged the Common Core State Standards conversations: 1) learning experts, 2) journalists, 3) K–12 teachers, 4) community members, 5) politicians, and 6) mixed groups. The positions taken on the topic were varied and divergent. Many from the right wing conservative front saw the Common Core Standards as big government takeover of schools and as an unconstitutional expansion of federal government control of schools. Those on the left wing saw it as the imposition of high-stakes testing, efforts to link student performance to teacher evaluations, and as subtle inroads to other reform measures such as school choice and the corporate takeover of schools.[22] Surprisingly, a 2014 survey revealed that 85 percent of Americans saw Common Core State Standards as a subtle way for the federal government to mine the personal data of citizens.

In 2012, 90 percent of Americans who were sampled favored the Common Core Standards, but in 2016 the favorability had declined to 50 percent.[23] As of May 2016, thirty-eight US states have abandoned either the SBAC or the PARCC consortium, with only six states committing to implement the PARCC. The total number of states planning to use the Common Core State Standards had dropped from its all-time height of forty-five in 2011 to twenty in 2016.[24] This is how much things changed. So, the story of the Common Core State Standards is a perfect example of the nature of the pushback that globalization is getting and its impact on the educational setting.

CONCLUSION

Globalization seems to have hit some obstacle courses in many parts of the Western world due to a rising tide of nativism in Europe and the United States. The fact remains that globalization has come to stay. The genie is out of the bottle. The information superhighway will not be stopped, international trade and commerce will not be halted, and the movement of people and goods across national boundaries will not be stopped, even with iron walls. Societies are better off rethinking their educational practices and invest into preparing their students to function effectively as global citizens, not just regional or local citizens.

Chapter Three

Federal Affirmative Action and Its Implications for Equal Educational Opportunities in the United States

CHAPTER OBJECTIVES

This chapter discusses the federal affirmative action programs in the United States and the implications they bear on educational opportunities for ethnic- and gender-minority people in the US population. Readers will be able to explore the history and purpose of federal affirmative action programs in education. They will examine and become familiar with the effects of the ban on affirmative action in education in many US states, and the various efforts and lawsuits that have aimed at ending affirmative action in education and their impact so far.

HISTORY AND PURPOSE OF AFFIRMATIVE ACTION IN THE UNITED STATES

Affirmative action in the United States is a government-based action aimed at providing opportunities for minorities in education and employment with the goal of remedying past ills of discrimination as well as fostering a healthy and more equitable society. The history of affirmative action must trace back to the US Supreme Court ruling in *Brown v. Board of Education*, which legally barred intentional discrimination and segregation in public schools.

The end of segregation of public schools meant that blacks, women, and other minorities could apply to go to any publicly owned K–12 higher educational institution and that they should be admitted without discrimination. Sadly, that was not the case following *Brown v. Board of Education*. American history shows that many colleges continued to make it hard for blacks and other minorities to gain admission, especially when standardized test scores that have been proved to be culturally biased toward the white middle class is used as admission criteria (Kearns, 2011; Kearns, 2016; and Goldberg, 2004).

For a nation that was just emerging from an educational policy of Separate but Equal, where educational opportunities were separate but not equal with blacks being educated in significantly substandard educational settings with very limited resources and textbooks that were ten or more years behind those being used in white schools, it was obvious that significant achievement gaps in education would exist, and yet specific actions were not taken to address these inequities.

Affirmative action in the United States was a tool aimed at fighting visible and entrenched discrimination on the basis of race and gender. Affirmative action calls for taking proactive measures to address and minimize the exclusion of women and ethnic minority individuals from employment, college admission, and other public opportunities.[1] Decades of discrimination and exclusionary actions made it imperative to face the reality that passivity would not end discrimination and its effects, so the United States government needed to take action to end discrimination in public opportunities. The origins of affirmative action date much earlier to 1941, long before *Brown v. Board of Education*, when President Franklin D. Roosevelt signed an executive order calling for a full and equitable participation of all Americans in the workforce without discrimination on the basis of race, creed, color, or nation of origin.

Landsberg (1995) posits that Roosevelt signed this executive order in response to the pressures from African American labor leaders who were clamoring for an end to discrimination in the workforce. Roosevelt's action is said to have started with an instruction to his National Defense Council to hire Negroes in the workforce based on quality instead of turning down a first-class Negro worker for a "3rd class white boy."[2] In this statement, Roosevelt called out the American society on what was a pervasive ill and practice in which the educational backgrounds of blacks and their professional skills were rendered inconsequential simply because of the color of their skin, and whites who were significantly underqualified would be hired in their place.

The post–*Brown v. Board of Education* version of affirmative action traces back to President Lyndon B. Johnson, who in 1965 signed an executive order requiring nondiscrimination and affirmative action in awarding federal contracts. Richard Nixon strengthened this order in 1969, when he imposed goals and timetables for the utilization of minority employees. Prior to both Johnson and Nixon's acts, however, there was the Title VII Civil Rights Act of 1964, whose goal was:

> To enforce the constitutional right to vote, to confer jurisdiction upon the district courts of the United States to provide injunctive relief against discrimination in public accommodations, to authorize the attorney general to institute suits to

protect constitutional rights in public facilities and public education, to extend the Commission on Civil Rights, to prevent discrimination in federally assisted programs, to establish a Commission on Equal Employment Opportunity, and for other purposes.[3]

While Title VII broadly addressed discrimination, there was the Title VI Civil Rights Act of 1964, which "prohibits discrimination on the basis of race, color, and national origin in programs and activities receiving federal financial assistance."[4] This law focused specifically on educational opportunities for minorities, in relation to how they were recruited, admitted, and offered financial assistance for college education.

Landsberg (1995) articulated the objectives of affirmative action in the following ways: First, as a reparative action to overcome the effects of past discrimination by individuals, the state, and the society at large. Second, as a prophylactic action to ensure against future discrimination. Third, to promote diversity in the educational setting (and, I would add, the workplace, but not necessarily the case with federal contractors). Fourth, to overcome the continuing effects of a two-class society characterized by racial division, and to provide for a fair share of the national pie to all the groups represented in the society.[5]

THE RELEVANCE OF AFFIRMATIVE ACTION IN THE UNITED STATES TODAY

Some fabrics of US society feel that affirmative action has outlived its usefulness today. Others have even taken the matter further to argue that affirmative action is not only outdated, but that it has become a basis for reverse discrimination against the white population. A few affirmative action programs have raised eyebrows and made people cry foul at the so-called attempt to end discrimination.

Some such arguments have been articulated in court cases involving the following institutions over the years: the University of Georgia, Louisiana State University, Southern University, Alabama State University, Maryland Higher Education Commission, the University of California, the University of Texas, and the University of Michigan.

In this section we will discuss a few prominent affirmative action cases that have challenged the legality of affirmative action in higher education admission, namely: the *Regents of the University of California v. Bakke* (1978), *Hopwood v. University of Texas* (1996), *Gratz v. Bollinger, et al.,* 2003, *Wooden v. the Board of Regents of the University of Georgia*, NAACP, 2001, and the case of Alabama State University.

The Regents of the *University of California v. Bakke* (1978)

The medical school at the University of California, Davis (UC Davis) had two admission criteria for the entering class of one hundred students. These were known as regular admission and special admission programs. The regular admission process denied admission to students with a grade point average below 2.5 on a 4.0 scale. The admission process considered also the grade point average on science courses, Medical College Admission Test (MCAT) scores, letters of recommendation, extracurricular activities, and other biographical data, including an interview rating that was generated by a university committee for one out of every six applicants. The full admissions committee made the final decisions on these general applications. A separate committee made up of majority minority members made decisions on the special admission program.

In 1973 and 1974, applicants who identified as educationally or economically disadvantaged and members of minority groups were considered under this special admission category. About one-fifth of these applicants were invited for an interview during this time period, and the top choices were forwarded to the admission committee to make the final decision on their admission. No disadvantaged white student was admitted under the special admission classification.

Over a four-year period, sixty-three minority students were admitted under the special admission category, and only forty-four under general admission. Allan Bakke, a thirty-five-year-old white male applied twice for admission into UC Davis and was denied admission both times. His qualifications, however, exceeded the qualifications (GPA and test scores) of the minority students admitted under the special admission criteria, and he filed a lawsuit alleging discrimination on the basis of race, since sixteen slots were reserved for minority groups who might not have met the general admission requirements, denying Bakke admission, even though he had met the general admission requirement. The court ruled that Bakke should be offered admission because the university could not prove that he would have been denied admission if not for the special admission requirements. The case was appealed by the Regent of the UC to the Supreme Court.

On June 26, 1978, four of the US Supreme Court justices held that the use of quota in admission violated the Civil Rights Act of 1964. Justice Lewis Powell, taking sides with four other justices who held that the use of race as a criterion in admissions decisions in higher education was constitutionally permissible, presented the plurality opinion. He argued that while the rigid use of racial quotas as it was employed at UC Davis violated the Equal Protection Clause of the Fourteenth Amendment, the use of race was permissible as one of several admission criteria.[6]

Justice Powell's argument provided the framework for examining affirmative action cases for the subsequent years. The framework required the following:

- There must be no rigid quota or functional equivalent in the form of a set-aside or predetermined number of seats for minorities.
- Minority applicants should not be reviewed under a separate admissions track that insulated them from non-minority applicants.
- Race should be one of several possible plus factors to be considered; other factors may include unique life experiences, challenges, interests or talents, socioeconomic disadvantage, or geography.
- Each applicant must be treated as an individual rather than a stand-in for a favored group.
- No specific racial or ethnic group should be singled out by the program; rather, the program should look to all racial and ethnic groups as contributing to genuine diversity.[7]

In effect, the court struck down the UC Davis admission policy as unconstitutional, based on the fact that it operated as a quota system, reserving certain slots for minorities. However, it allowed the use of race as a factor (among many other factors) for admission decisions under limited circumstances. It prevented institutions from using race-conscious policies to remedy past discrimination, but it permitted its use toward the achievement of a diverse student body.[8]

In 1995, the California Board of Regents voted to pass Special Policy 1 (SP-1), which banned the use of race as a factor in admission in any UC system. In 1997, the policy was amended to also apply to professional and graduate school admissions in the UC system. This means that for the University of California system, the use of affirmative action in admission decisions ended effectively in 1997.[9]

Hopwood v. University of Texas (1996)

The case of *Hopwood v. University of Texas* pertains to the use of race as a factor in law school admissions. Cheryl J. Hopwood, Douglas W. Carwell, Kenneth R. Elliot, and David A. Rogers were all non-minority Texas residents who applied for admission into the University of Texas Law School for the 1992–1993 academic year. The law school used affirmative action in admission decisions. The action was aimed at achieving diversity and overcoming past effects of discrimination.

In 1992–1993 admissions, decisions were made for general admission by a full admissions committee. A minority subcommittee also participated in making decisions on minority applicants based on what they called the Texas Index (TI). Decision on minority applicants utilized a lower admissions standard based on the TI, but each applicant was given extensive consideration from all three members of the minority subcommittee if it fell into what was considered a discretionary zone.

This committee made the admission decision for minority students in the discretionary zone, but for nonminority students in the discretionary zone, those receiving two or more votes were admitted, and those with one vote were placed on an admission waiting list, while those with no vote were denied admission.[10]

While Elliott, Carvell, and Rogers each had a TI of 197, placing them on the high end of the discretionary zone for resident nonminority students, Hopwood had an undergraduate GPA of 3.8 with an LSAT score of 39, making a TI of 199. This placed this candidate on the low end of the presumptive admit category for resident nonminority applicants. Both groups were denied admission, and they filed a lawsuit in the US District Court claiming that affirmative action violated the Equal Protection Clause of the Fourteenth Amendment. The district court judged the admission process as unconstitutional because it treated minorities as a separate class.

The University system appealed the ruling to the Fifth Circuit Court of Appeals, and the higher court upheld the ruling of the lower court, affirming that the practice was unconstitutional. They determined that the achievement of diversity as well as remedying the effects of past discrimination were not compelling reasons to justify the use of race as a factor for admission decisions.[11]

The University of Texas appealed the ruling to the US Supreme Court, but the Supreme Court declined to hear the case, and this meant that the lower court ruling stood. The decision on *Hopwood v. Texas* had implications for all the states served by the US Fifth Circuit Court, namely Texas, Louisiana, and Mississippi. All these states were barred from using racial preference in the admissions decision process since this court ruling in 1996. The University of Texas was able to increase the number of minority students admitted into their system without violating the constitution, by offering automatic admission to any Texas state university to anyone (minority or nonminority) who graduated in the top 10 percent from a Texas high school.[12]

Gratz v. Bollinger, et al.

Gratz v. Bollinger, et al. includes two class-action lawsuits filed in the fall of 1997 by the Center for Individual Rights[13] on behalf of white students who had been denied admission into the undergraduate programs of the University of Michigan as well as into the University of Michigan Law School. The allegation was that the university utilized different test scores and grade point averages for admission decisions concerning white students from the ones they used for minority students.

The University of Michigan's College of Literature, Science and Arts would usually receive a high volume of applications. To manage these applications, they implemented a point-based system for admissions, which rated students with points from 1 to 100. Using this system, a student from an underrepresented group automatically received 20 points while extraordinarily talented and artistic students received 5 points toward their overall points.

In 1995, Jennifer Gratz applied to the University of Michigan College of Literature, Science and Arts. Her adjusted grade point average was 3.8, and her ACT score was 25. She was denied admission. In 1997, another white student—Patrick Hamacher—applied with a GPA of 3.0 and ACT score of 28. He was also denied admission. These two individuals were both within the minimum requirements for admission into the college, but given that there was a limited space each year, not all qualified candidates would be given admission. They were among others who were otherwise qualified, but denied admission.

In October 1997, the two filed a lawsuit alleging that the university's use of racial preference in undergraduate admission decisions violated the Equal Protection Clause of the Fourteenth Amendment and the Title VI of the Civil Rights Act of 1964. They were seeking compensatory and punitive damages for past violations, alleging that the respondents violated their rights to nondiscriminatory treatment. They sought an injunction prohibiting the university from continuing to discriminate on the basis of race, and to offer them an admission as transfer students.[14]

In a 2000 district court ruling, Judge Patrick Duggan ruled that the admission system under which the two plaintiffs were denied admission was unconstitutional, but upheld the admission system in place, which went into effect in 1999 as tailored well to advance government interest in attaining diversity. The plaintiffs appealed the case to the US Sixth Circuit Court of Appeal. This case, as well as another case involving the University of Michigan filed December 1997 by another white student, made their way to the US Supreme Court, which heard the cases on April 1, 2003, and reached a decision on June 23, 2003.

In its decision, the US Supreme Court held that the university's use of racial preferences in admission decisions violated both the Equal Protection Clause and Title VI Civil Rights Act. They argued that granting automatic 20 points to underrepresented minority applicants was based solely on race and did not constitute individualized consideration.

On the Grutter case, which pertained to law school admission, the court held that given the fact that the law school conducted a highly individualized review of applicants, no case could be made based exclusively on race, so the Equal Protection Clause could not have been violated. According to Justice Powell, racial and ethnic origin is a single but important element for consideration in order to meet the university's desire for a diverse student body.[15]

Wooden v. the Board of Regents of the University of Georgia, NAACP (2001)

Up until 1999, various discrimination lawsuits were filed by different individuals against the University of Georgia (UGA). The plaintiffs claimed that the university's admission system, both in the past and in the present, used racially discriminatory admission criteria for white and black applicants. They claimed that at the state's three historically black universities, the admission system implemented two different criteria, one for whites and one for blacks, and that the practice was discriminatory against whites.

A 1997 case filed by a white applicant on this basis was dismissed by a district court because the court determined that the white applicant (Greene) lacked the necessary combination of grades, test scores, and other required elements to qualify for admission. This, along with a number of other cases, was dismissed by a district court on the basis that the plaintiffs had not suffered any injury. These cases, however, were later consolidated and appealed in 1999 and together they were finally decided in 2001. Among these cases was Tracy, Davis, and Greene, unsuccessful applicants to the University of Georgia who claimed that the freshman admissions policies favored nonwhites over whites, and violated the Equal Protection Clause and federal civil rights policies.

Part of the Supreme Court decision on this matter reads as follows:

UGA is the flagship institution of Georgia's university system. Admission to UGA is competitive, and applications far exceed the number of available freshman seats. To assemble a class, the faculty admission committee, in conjunction with the admissions office, recommends a freshman admission policy each year. This policy is formally presented to UGA's president for approval, and thereafter is implemented by the admissions office. From 1990 to 1995, UGA's freshman admissions policy applied objective academic criteria differently depending upon whether an applicant characterized himself as "black" or "nonblack." To be eligible for admission, an applicant had to meet certain pre-set minimums with respect to Scholastic Aptitude Test ("SAT") score, grade point average ("GPA"), and academic index ("AI"). Under the 1990–95 policy, the minimums for black students were set lower than the minimums for non-black students. Specifically, to be eligible for admission into the fall 1995 class, a black applicant would have to obtain at least an 800 SAT score, a 2.0 GPA, and a 2.0 academic index. By contrast, a non-black applicant would have to obtain at least a 980 SAT score, a 2.5 GPA, and a 2.4 academic index. This was the regime when plaintiff Kirby Tracy (who is white) applied for admission to UGA's fall 1995 Class. Tracy had a GPA of 3.47 and a total SAT score of 830. Because he did not meet the minimum SAT requirement for non-blacks, UGA denied his application. It is undisputed, however, that Tracy would have been eligible for admission under the criteria applied to black applicants.[16]

In the part of this case that pertained to Tracy, Davis, and Greene, the Supreme Court upheld the lower court ruling dismissing the claims of discrimination based on the fact that the plaintiffs did not meet the required admission criteria.

Alabama State University

In 1995, a federal judge ordered each of two historically black universities, Alabama State University and Alabama A&M University, to spend up to $1 million each year for ten years in funding scholarships for exclusively white students. Between 1996 and 1997, the scholarships awarded to white students at these schools amounted to 40 percent of their grant money. This meant that all the white students at these schools had their tuition, fees, and room and board fully covered by scholarship money, and all they needed to qualify for this money was a grade of C.

In 1997, a black student sued for discrimination because he was denied money from this scholarship. The suit also claimed that black students were held to a higher standard at these institutions in order to qualify for scholarship. In response to this lawsuit, Alabama State University raised the eligibility standards for white students, as well.[17]

EXAMPLES OF AFFIRMATIVE ACTION OUTSIDE THE UNITED STATES

It is important to note that affirmative action is not an exclusively American idea. Many countries of the world that have recognized the lasting effects of discrimination and the competitive disadvantage faced by many minority groups in many societies have taken steps to reduce discrimination as well as remedy the ills that resulted from previous policies and practices that fostered discrimination. Federal and state Brazilian universities use quotas to recruit racial minority, poor, and handicapped applicants into the universities. The

University of Palmares (Unipalmares) reserves 50 percent of its slots for Brazillian blacks, "reflecting the fact that roughly half the country's 183 million people have African slaves as forefathers."[18]

Canadian affirmative action is more blatantly skewed in favor of minorities. Both in employment and college admission, the Canadian aboriginal groups and other minorities are given preference for jobs and educational opportunities in a three-tier system that classifies the aboriginals as P1, women and other minority groups as P2, and white men as P3. In Finland, there are quotas reserved for Swedish-speaking applicants into the legal and medical fields. These are just a few of many countries that have affirmative action policies.[19]

A 2009 article by Jane Onsongo (2009) provided a detailed discussion of affirmative action in three African countries: Kenya, Uganda, and Tanzania. In Kenya, the educational system consists of two years of early childhood education, eight years of primary school education, four years of secondary school education, and four years of university education.

At the end of their secondary school education, Kenyan students take the Kenya Certificate of Secondary Education (KCSE) examination, and a passing grade of C+ is required for university admission. Between 2000 and 2004, females made up only 22 percent of students in the undergraduate programs in Kenya, and only 5 percent of students in the graduate and postgraduate institutions. The Kenyan government has taken actions to address the underrepresentation of girls in their secondary and tertiary institutions by adopting affirmative action policies that tend to promote the increase of girls' enrollment in the secondary and tertiary institutions.[20]

The same study showed that girls made up 45.5 percent of the enrollment in Ugandan secondary schools, and 34 percent of university students. Uganda has also used a combination of factors of affirmative action and the provision of sanitary and supportive learning environments to attract more girls into her primary and secondary schools. A stand-alone ministry of Gender, Labor and Social Development has been established to engage gender equity in employment (and university admissions).

In Tanzania, 37.7 percent of university students are females, 21 percent of master's degree students, and 18.9 percent of Ph.D. students as of the year 2008 were females. The Tanzanian constitution bans discrimination on any basis. A national strategy for overcoming gender inequity has been identified as Gender Mainstreaming. There are clear guidelines for achieving gender equity and for facilitating upward mobility for females in education and employment. It should be evident, therefore, that striving for equity requires that special consideration be given to the population of people who have previously suffered discrimination and have been deprived of opportunities whether in America, in Brazil, or in Uganda.

THE EFFECTS OF THE BAN ON AFFIRMATIVE ACTION IN EDUCATION IN THE UNITED STATES

Over the years, the combined forces of legal challenges, legislative actions, court decisions, and executive actions have had a lasting effect on the viability of affirmative action in the United States. While some court decisions have conceded to the fact that affirmative action may be educationally appropriate in certain contexts to promote a diverse student population where diversity is considered a compelling educational factor, the Supreme Court made it clear in the Bakke decision that diversity may not be a compelling educational interest.

One of the factors that has worked against affirmative action in the United States is the fact that when reference is made to affirmative action, people tend to conclude that it refers exclusively to giving African Americans unmerited access to university admissions, to the detriment of qualifying white counterparts. What is often not considered is the fact that affirmative action goes beyond race to gender and socioeconomic conditions. Also, affirmative action calls for admission requirements that take into consideration factors that go beyond standardized test scores.

Research has often proven that standardized tests are both ethnically and socioeconomically biased in many cases.[21] Affirmative action seeks to provide broader criteria for admissions in the context of research-based problems of significant achievement gaps that have existed in the United States due to the combined forces of discrimination, poverty, and limited access to quality educational experiences to ethnic minority people. Data provided by the Association of American Medical Colleges shows that the average Medical College Admission Test (MCAT) scores of black, Hispanic, or Native American applicants are usually lower than those of white applicants.

These differences are not indicative of any innate deficiencies in intelligence or learning faculties; rather, they reflect disparities in socioeconomic backgrounds as well as white cultural scripts that these tests are often written in, which may be alien to these nonwhite test takers.[22] To rely exclusively on standardized test scores in making admission decisions would disproportionately undermine the chances of nonwhite socioeconomically disadvantaged applicants, many of whom have exhibited great skill and intellectual prowess when the opportunity has been given to them to enroll in medical and other professional schools.[23]

For the meantime, it appears that the US courts have affirmed the importance of diversity, allowing the use of group identity as a factor in university admission decisions, yet the use of this factor has been significantly limited to ensure its constitutionality, requiring that admission policies using diversity as a criteria must not focus on a single group in theory or in practice.[24]

A number of executive actions that have attempted to limit the effects of affirmative action can be found at both the federal and state levels of the US government. During his presidency, Bill Clinton ordered a review of federal affirmative action, in which his administration announced that while it would continue to support measures that promote opportunities for minorities in employment, education, and government contracts, programs must be eliminated or reformed if they create quotas, create preferences for unqualified individuals, create reverse discrimination, or continue to exist even after their equal opportunity purpose has been achieved.

About the same time that this was happening at the federal level, Governor Pete Wilson of California repealed various executive actions that had required affirmative action in the state, mandating government agencies to eliminate all affirmative action programs that had not been mandated by federal or state laws.[25] In 1999, Florida governor Jeb Bush issued an executive order that effectively ended racial and gender preferences in university admission, employment, and contracting, through what he called One Florida Initiative.[26]

In 1996, California voters approved California Affirmative Action Proposition 209. This proposition amended California constitution by prohibiting public institutions from "discriminating on the basis of race, sex, or ethnicity."[27] While this proposition reads as though it is positively disposed toward affirmative action, the assumption here is that affirmative action is discriminatory against those who are not of minority status, so this law essentially abolished affirmative action's use in admission decisions in the state universities. Legal challenges were mounted against this law, but the US Supreme Court upheld the law as constitutional.

The consequence of the passage of Proposition 209 in California is that years after its passage, the minority admission into California's most prestigious universities has declined. African American and Latino admissions into state colleges such as UC Berkeley and UC San Diego have both fallen dramatically.[28] Between 1995 and 2010, while the percentage of white students enrolled in UC Berkeley or UCLA has increased or remained the same, the percentage of African American freshmen at both prestigious UCs have fallen by 40 to 45 percent.[29]

The cumulative effects of the bans on affirmative action across the nation has led to a drop of 1.2 percentage points in the enrollment of students of color into graduate programs, placing minority students at merely 8.75 percent of graduate school enrollments (Garces, 2012). The enrollment of minority students in the fields of engineering dropped by 1.6 percent, natural sciences dropped by 1.5 percent, social sciences by 1.9 percent, and education by 2 percent. One wonders why this kind of decrease in opportunities is desirable in a democracy like the United States.[30]

The state of Colorado, with its predominantly white population, still felt threatened by affirmative action, and a movement to repeal it in Colorado in 2008 nearly won the battle. In 2005, undergraduate students who identified themselves as white constituted 72 percent of enrollment in Colorado colleges and universities, African Americans comprised 1.4 percent, Latinos 6.3 percent, and Asians were 6.4 percent. Colorado's Amendment 46[31] lost when 50.7 percent of the voters voted against it and 49.2 percent voted for it. Considering the impact that California's Proposition 209 has had on college admissions into California state universities, one can only imagine what the passage of this amendment would have meant for minority applicants into Colorado colleges and universities.[32]

THE CASE OF WHITE AFFIRMATIVE ACTION

It must be noted, however, that while much opposition has been mounted against affirmative action as a criterion for admission into US colleges on the basis that it gives undue advantage to ethnic minorities, there seems to be a dearth of similar opposition to other measures that seem to favor the rich and white population more disproportionally. One such measure addresses alumni benefits, or what is called legacy admission in most universities. This is a process by which an applicant whose parent attended the same institution is given preferential consideration over those whose parents did not.

In a 2005 study by Espenshade and Chung, legacy status gave applicants a 160-point upswing on their SAT scores. The same study revealed that legacy criteria disproportionately favors whites and Asians over Hispanics and African Americans.[33] A Harvard University researcher studied thirty elite colleges in the United States in 2011 and revealed that the children of undergraduate alumni, otherwise known as "primary legacies," were more likely to get admitted into elite schools than their counterparts who are not legacy children.

According to this study, while legacy applicants were given a 23.3 percentage-point increase in their admission criteria points, "primary legacies" received 45.1 percentage points. The study further highlights that while a non-legacy applicant may face a 15 percent chance of getting in, a primary legacy would have a 60 percent chance of getting in.[34] Given that minority people were historically discriminated from admission into these prestigious schools for decades before affirmative action, only those applicants who come from the group that has known privilege and opportunities all along will likely qualify for legacy admissions. So, in effect, the practice of giving preferential treatment to privileged white groups has continued while some are crying foul at the use of affirmative action to increase opportunities for minorities.

The fact is that, even after the implementation of affirmative action, college admission has continued to favor whites in a larger percentage, since one can deduce that legacy criteria is not likely to benefit minority applicants as it would white and wealthy applicants. The question that has not been asked and dealt with is whether legacy admission criteria amounts to discrimination against ethnic minorities and the poor over the rich and white population. It is a conversation that must be had if we will continue to question the constitutionality of the use of affirmative action in university admissions.

Another set of admission criteria that has not received enough critical examination include state-based preferences, preferences for athletes, military backgrounds, and in some cases geographical considerations, such as special considerations given to applicants from the Appalachian regions. The question is not raised to dispute the validity of these criteria as justifiable in giving opportunities to people from regions and classes that are disadvantaged by poverty or career military decisions, but rather the question is raised as to why these other considerations are not getting as much pushback as affirmative action is, whose goal is to provide opportunities for groups that have previously suffered government sanctioned discriminations that left negative generational impacts that continue to be felt in many families and communities today.

Chapter Four

Global Issues on Gender Equity

CHAPTER OBJECTIVES

This chapter presents the various issues that have limited women's rights across the globe over the centuries. It investigates the history and development of women's rights at a global level, as well as the battle for gender equality in various parts of the world. It addresses issues of poverty and women's rights violations in various parts of the world. Readers will be able to grasp the various ways women's rights have been limited over the centuries at a global level: in the United States, the Middle East, and African countries. They will engage in a discussion of the struggles for women's rights in various parts of the world, along with movements and initiatives that have shaped the struggle for women's rights at a global level. Also, the many continuing areas of gender inequity across the world will be highlighted.

INTRODUCTION

The advancement of women's rights and the push for gender equity as a global movement gained some momentum during the civil rights era in the United States. By the 1970s, attention was focused on the rights of women within political institutions as well as the distribution of publicly owned resources toward advancing the rights of women (Conrad, Dixon, and Green, 2014). During this time, public policies and educational curricula were analyzed to expose obvious and implicit gender biases, and to explore remedies to these biases. The 1970s saw an upsurge in women's studies programs just as the same was happening in the areas of ethnic studies (African studies, Hispanic studies, and others).

While the conversation on women's rights was beginning to gain steam in certain circles, many countries and corporations were slow in coming along. African countries that were beginning to emerge from colonialism seemed to have more urgent things to focus on. Arab nations were almost all closed up to any meaningful engagement with issues of gender equity. China, practically operating outside of the global economic family of nations with a strong communist agenda, was practically opposed to any dialogue on gender issues. The engine of change was moving rather slowly in many parts of the world.

Globalization, and its accompanying revolutions in communication, economics, and transportation, has been credited in certain circles with propelling issues of gender equity to the forefront of global conversations. Lindsey (2013), however, argues that even within the context of globalization and its accompanying issues, gender equity has been marginalized from the larger conversation on globalization. As the conversation on gender equity proceeds in this book, efforts will be made to explore the forms in which the struggle for gender equity has taken in many countries, especially non-Western nations. Global efforts at advancing gender equity made within the context of the United Nations structures will be highlighted and explored.

CONTEMPORARY ISSUES ON THE EDUCATION OF WOMEN ACROSS THE GLOBE

In the year 2004, a study by Herz and Sperling[1] revealed that sixty million girls from age six to eleven do not attend school in various parts of the world. Another one hundred million are said to drop out of school before they are able to finish their elementary school education. These girls are mostly hindered from pursuing education due to cultural and traditional practices and worldviews, as well as government policies that tend to stack up against them. They are systemically excluded from the opportunities that come through the attainment of a good education. This is the height of social exclusion.

Social inclusion is the process by which those who are at risk of poverty and social exclusion gain opportunities and resources they need to fully participate in the economic, social, and cultural life of society. It ensures that persons who are excluded are able to enjoy a standard of living and well-being that would be considered normal in the society in which they live. It speaks to a social policy of engagement and opportunities for participation in society as a means to improve the quality of life of otherwise marginalized individuals and to reduce social isolation.[2]

Women from across the globe have historically been excluded from participation in the normal life of societies for ages, rather than be included.

These exclusions have come as a result of factors such as cultural and traditional views of women that are often discriminatory, cultural and traditional views of gender roles, and national policies that tend to inhibit the chances of women to rise beyond their marginalized states.

A recent study of Pakistani Mirpuri immigrants to Great Britain revealed an overwhelming positive response of parents toward the education of their daughters. While 38 percent of the fathers interviewed responded positively to the need for the education of their daughters and 71 percent of the mothers also responded positively to the same, when asked about sending their own daughters to British schools, they were a little less inclined to do so, based on concerns about sending their girls to schools where boys and girls mix openly, and to exposing their daughters to the corruption of Western value systems such as unbridled freedom and independence, extramarital sex, and other practices that conflict with Islamic religious and social norms.[3]

One can see how strongly cultural and religious values and traditions still impede Muslim girls' access to education, even in Western societies. This is the twenty-first century, yet women are still having to deal with these issues, even in Western societies.

In his 2007 historical novel, *A Thousand Splendid Suns*, Khaled Hosseini[4] portrays the continuing injustices against women in the Muslim countries of Afghanistan and Pakistan, which range from the denial of Western education to forced marriages and the inability to travel without a male escort. While it is unquestionable that women's rights have been advanced significantly in the past two decades, the inability of women to enjoy equal rights with men on a number of fronts remain major concerns worldwide.

There are certain human rights that have been clearly identified as inalienable to all humans regardless of gender, ethnicity, and country of origin. These rights include the right to personal safety; the right to basic health care, education, employment opportunities, a fair wage, a voice or vote in the political process; and the right to property ownership. While progress has been made on women's access to these basic human needs in the United States, women continue to lag behind men in all of these areas at a global level.

More women than men live in poverty worldwide. Take for instance a February 25, 2015, article on *INFORMILO*, titled, "The Networked Economy: How Technology, Innovation and Venture Capital Are Transforming the Future of Mobile."[5] The article indicates that while mobile phone ownership has skyrocketed worldwide in the past few years, women are said to be 21 percent less likely to own a mobile phone than men. The report said that this gap gets wider if that woman lives in Africa, the Middle East, or South Asia. This is essentially due to the income gap that exists between women in these areas and women in developed countries.

According to Sheykhjan, Rajeswari, and Jabari (2014), gender equity is no longer viewed solely as a social justice issue; rather, it is also widely recognized as essential to societal growth and development.[6] Education is said to be the social equalizer in any society, yet women across the globe have been denied equal access to education over the years. Muslim women are particularly underrepresented in schools, and especially in higher education all over the world (Oplatka and Lapidot, 2012).[7]

In the twenty-first century, education is the most important tool to help break a persistent pattern of gender discrimination and bring about a lasting change that favors women across the globe (Sheykhjan, Rajeswari, and Jabari, 2014). In the United States, for example, the percentage of women who attained an undergraduate education in 2015 was not statistically different from that of men, with women at 33 percent who achieve an undergraduate education slightly edging out the 32 percent that men attained in undergraduate enrollment (Ryan and Bauman, 2016).[8]

In Pakistan, while the literacy rate among men is 61.7 percent, the rate among women is 35.2 percent. In rural areas, the percentage for female literacy drops even further to 25 percent, while the drop in the enrollment of girls in schools falls to 50 percent. A primary reason for the low literacy rate for females and the low enrollment of girls in schools is said to be gender biases that are rampant in curriculum, textbooks, and the cultural norms of the society (Latif, 2009).[9]

Pakistani girls receive an average of only 2.5 years of schooling, while boys receive five years on the average. Other studies show that primary school completion rate for girls in rural Pakistan is three times lower than that of boys in the same areas.[10] In Pakistan, a combination of cultural and traditional worldviews, colonial influences, and the prevalence of Islam has led to a gender perspective in which women's roles in society are limited to reproduction, managing domestic chores, rearing children, and cooking and cleaning (Latif, 2009).

The Pakistani society tends to see the woman as an emotional partner to the man; she has limited understanding, no mind, no voice, and is simply a sexual object. Parents in Pakistan save money to get their girls married off rather than saving money to put them through school. Girls are married off as soon as they reach puberty so their parents can be relieved of the duties of taking care of them, and instead concentrate on raising the boys into men.

In Egypt, the adult literacy of men between the years 1997 and 2007 was 74.6 percent, while the literacy rate for women was 57.8 percent. While Egypt could be said to be more progressive than Pakistan, the rate of female literacy in Egypt remains low. In 2004, 4.8 percent more boys were enrolled in secondary schools than girls. This meant that the percentage of girls who would have access to higher education would be even lower.[11]

The perception of women has changed over time in Egypt. During the early days of Egyptian independence from Great Britain, Egypt had a large number of educated men and women. The celebration of the "Unveiled Women" in the 1930s culminated a strong support of the public presence and participation of women in Egyptian life (Megahed and Lack, 2011).

This progress in women's rights, however, has been significantly eroded in the past few decades due to a growing reaffirmation of the traditional roles of women in Egyptian society, which has come mostly from the resurgence of fundamentalist Muslim groups such as the Muslim Brotherhood. There were many confrontations between those who are for (Egyptian government) and those who are against (Islamists) women's rights in Egypt between the 1990s and the year 2010 (and even more recently following the Arab uprising). These often involved schoolgirls and the *hijab* (head covering or veil) or the *'niqab* (face veil).

While these tensions have persisted, they have not negatively impacted the chances of women's enrollment in Egyptian schools (Megahed & Lack, 2011).[12] Despite advances in Egypt, a 2009 Global Gender Gap Report ranked Egypt 126th in the 2009 Global Gender Gap Index. By 2013, Egypt was still at 125th, essentially the same ranking four years later (Global Gender Gap Report, 2013).[13]

The Nigerian societies, on the other hand, enjoyed a positive effect of colonialism, which touted education as a ladder for opportunities. While the Nigerian societies valued and embraced Western education, boys were offered more opportunities for educational attainment than girls. The inequity between boys' and girls' opportunities to attend school stem from a combination of cultural and economic factors.

Education in the Nigerian setting was mostly pay as you go, so parents invested much into the education of their children. Being an egalitarian society, where male children tended to be valued more than female children, families often invested more in the education of their boys than their girls. The traditional view of women in most Nigerian societies was that they were homemakers, farmhands, child bearers, and subordinate to males.[14]

Data reveals that while the educational gap between Nigerian men and women remains wide in favor of men, Nigerian women have, however, made significant progress in educational attainment in recent years. Nigerian schools, from elementary school to institutions of higher learning, have a healthy ratio of women-to-men enrollment. A recent year's of average schooling data that compares male and female enrollment is provided (see Table 4.1.).

Table 4.1. Average Schooling Data for Nigeria

Characteristics	Mean Number of Years of Schooling	
Age	Men	Women
15-19	9.2	7.2
20-24	9.5	5.9
25-29	7.5	6.6
30-34	6.8	5.8
35-39	7.2	6.8
40-44	5.6	4.3
45-49	4.5	3.4
Residence		
Urban	6.7	6.9
Rural	4.6	3.8
Region		
North Central	6.3	4.2
North East	4.2	2.4
North West	3.5	1.7
South East	6.9	7.6
South South	7.9	6.8
South West	7.2	6.9

The Nigerian government institutions and establishments employ a healthy proportion of women and men. Nigeria has produced female university presidents (vice chancellors), speakers of state houses of representatives, federal ministers, and deputy governors. Incidentally, most of these women have come from the Christian Southern regions, where women's education is looked upon more favorably, compared to the Muslim North. Nigeria has made a steady progress on the Global Gender Gap Report since 2010:

2010 – 118th place
2011 – 120th place
2012 – 110th place
2013 – 106th place

Moving on to Tunisia, in North Africa, in response to the Beijing Conference on women (1995), the Tunisian government in its national action plan indicated that women have been the major victims of illiteracy in Tunisia. They came up with a national plan of action to combat this problem with the goal of lowering illiteracy among Tunisian women from 30 percent in 1992 to 17.3 percent in 1997. Tunisia may have made more progress than any other Muslim nation on the reduction of illiteracy among women in recent years.

The rate of female pre-university enrollment in Tunisia in 2005/2006 was 97.1 percent. This rose to 98.5 percent in the 2009/2010 year. In July 2002, Tunisia declared free educational opportunities for all citizens regardless of gender, origin, skin color, or religion.[15] Tunisia leaves a worthy example for other Muslim nations.

In China, the government has invested in the past five decades into the education of women. The goal, however, under a Chinese socialist government, is not to provide these women with opportunities for personal advancement, but rather it is done as a way to benefit the state. So educational opportunities for women is not so much a human rights issue as it is a state rights issue (Zhao, 2011). So while we record ongoing improvements in educational opportunities across the globe, some countries remain opposed to or uncommitted to the self-development of their women through education.

WOMEN'S POLITICAL AND CIVIL RIGHTS ISSUES AND MOVEMENTS

Traditions, worldviews, and cultural stereotypes remain major sources of hindrance to women's rights on a global level. Both developed and underdeveloped countries have their cultural attitudes, prejudices, and stereotypes toward women that are not empowering. More often than not, these traditions, beliefs, and practices lead to the denial of access to education, health care, property rights, employment, and decision-making powers to women in these societies.

In Pakistan, for example, there is a deeply rooted belief and custom that sees women as made exclusively for reproduction, homemaking, and child rearing. The woman is seen as an "emotional counterpart of man with much less understanding of the world. She does not have a mind and voice of her own, and is treated as a sexual object."[16]

The cultural norms in Pakistan oppress women. The dowry system often prevents parents from putting their children through school. Instead, they save up money for their girls' marriages and often force these young girls into early marriage, so as to relieve themselves of the burden of caring for them (Latif, 2009).[17] In African traditional societies, women were mostly responsible for doing farmwork and carrying out much of the agricultural production, in addition to being wives and mothers, cooks, and caregivers. Yet, society assigned them a subordinate role to men in every sphere of life.[18]

In the twenty-first century, gender equity is no longer viewed as a strictly social justice issue; rather, it is now seen as an essential ingredient to a society's growth and general development. "No country can fully develop economically and socially if it fails to tap and fully utilize the talent of its citizens."[19]

The argument is that when women have more control over resources, they are bound to spend more on basic living needs such as food, health care, and education, and this will positively impact society. Female education, they argue, has been proven by research to reduce female fertility rates, lower infant and child mortality rates, reduce maternal mortality rates, increase women's participation in the labor force, and foster educational investment in children (Sheykhjan, Rajeswari, and Jabari, 2014).

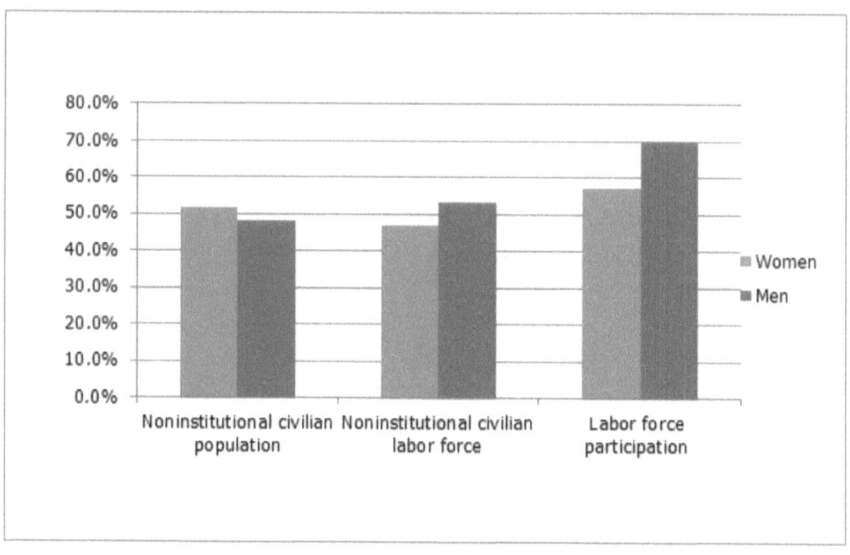

Figure 4.1. Population and Labor Force Participation by Sex

Research[20] has identified basic human rights to include food, health care, education, job opportunities, fair wages, a political voice, voting rights, and the right to property ownership. Human rights will not be worth the name if women's rights are excluded from the list. Unfortunately, women have fought for these basic rights in perpetuity, and yet men in many societies continue to hinder them from fully attaining these rights.

In the next section, we will explore the various forms the struggles for women's rights have taken in different societies. We will begin with a discussion of women's rights in Egypt and Tunisia, basing that discussion on the work of Megahed and Lack (2011). We will also discuss women's rights battles in Eastern Nigeria, known as the Women's War or Aba Women's Riot. We will end with a discussion of women liberation movements in the United States.

The Case with Egypt and Tunisia

Megahed and Lack (2011) identified three forces that have influenced women's rights in Egypt and Tunisia, as well as in many other Arab countries. These are 1) Islamic teaching and local traditions about women, 2) European colonial perceptions of women's rights, and 3) national gender-related policy reforms. While both cultural and religious teachings of Islam tend to assign the woman a secondary and invisible role in Islamic societies, there seems to be a divide among some Muslim scholars as to the rights of women to education.

There are those who interpret the Islamic laws as assigning women the right to higher levels of education, the right to property ownership, the right to engage in trade or professional activities, and the right to vote and to serve in political offices. These rights are said to be granted to women by Islam, yet most of them have not ever been implemented.[21] One of the areas of tension among Muslims has been the place of the *hijab* (head cover) in the lives of Muslim women.

While Westerners tend to look at the *hijab* with a Judeo-Christian and Western bias, some Muslim women have taken it to signify for them a symbol of political protest and rejection of the Western cultures. They tend to see it as a "combination of both submission to God's will and resistance of Western culture."[22] Traditional Arab and Muslim gender roles conflict with modern Western female roles, and as such the *hijab* offers Muslim women a clear distinction between the unveiled Western woman and the veiled Muslim woman.

The meaning of the *hijab*, however, is said to have changed from being purely a religious act to a symbol of cultural and political defiance.[23] One researcher states that the Muslim woman cannot be understood in the absence of her community, which is determined not just by geographic or social location, but which is a community conditioned by a shared faith.[24] In Egypt, however, society has never strictly enforced the *hijab*. In the 1930s, both men and women celebrated the "Unveiled Woman," promoting the public presence and participation of the woman in public life. Egyptian writers and politicians are said to have looked upon the education and equality of women as necessary for social advancement.

In 1979, an Egyptian law granting women the right to marriage, divorce, custody, and other civil rights was implemented by a presidential decree. That same year, another law made changes to women's representation in the parliament. In the 1980s, however, women lost some of these rights due to renewed opposition from the Islamists. Egypt appointed her first female judge in 2003, and in 2005 Egyptian women's divorce rights were expanded. An attempt, however, to amend a law that required women to obtain their husband's permission to travel was unsuccessful.[25]

In Tunisia, women seem to have made more progress than in any other Muslim country. Tunisia became the first Muslim nation to abolish polygamy. This was as far back as 1957. The government of Tunisia based this decision upon an injunction from Sharia law, which mandates that a man must treat all of his wives equally. The state argued that since it is humanly impossible for a man to do this, polygamy must be discouraged. Abortion rights were legislated in Tunisia in 1973, allowing abortions to take place up to the third month of pregnancy. The *hijab* was abolished in Tunisia in 1986, and the Tunisia government forbids the wearing of the *hijab* in government offices.[26] Between 2011 and 2016, the ban was partially lifted.

Aba Women's Riot (The Case for Nigeria)

While Nigeria can be described to be an egalitarian society, it remains at the same time an essentially male chauvinistic society. Men tend to wield much more power than women in politics, religion, trade, and industry. The Nigerian woman could be said in the traditional setting to be submissive and oftentimes subservient. As an individual, she tends to possess limited power and authority, but Nigerian women as a collective entity seem to wield much more power than is often acknowledged. The Women's War, or what has also been called the Aba Women's Riot, makes this case very clearly.

Igbo women of southeastern Nigeria, while submissive to their husbands and compliant homemakers, were not known to be pushovers. They were farmers, traders, and authorities in their own rights. As the British colonial rule was taking shape in Nigeria following the amalgamation of the northern and southern protectorates of Nigeria into one Nigerian colonial government in 1914, Sir Frederick Luggard, the colonial administrator, had instituted warrant chiefs in parts of Igbo land.

While the Calabar regions and other parts of the southeastern coast of the Atlantic were known to have kings and rulers, the Igbos were governed by an autonomous system of village and town administrations that were completely democratic. They did not have kings and chiefs, nor did they desire them. Luggard, however, thought it prudent to institute what he called warrant chieftaincy over the people, and chiefs were appointed for towns and villages. Often these chiefs were the least qualified for leadership in the community, but either because they could speak the English language and communicate well with the British administrators, or because they had other forms of access to the colonial rulers, they were appointed.

These chiefs, knowing they were neither elected by the people nor accountable to them, soon began to abuse their powers. While Igbo men, Efik men, and men from the other ethnic groups in eastern Nigeria suffered through the unending burdens of forced colonial labor, ever-increasing taxation, and corrupt local officials, levies, and much more, the case was different when the British administration decided to impose taxation on market women in eastern Nigeria. Fearing the impact such taxes could have on their trade and income, the women organized and raised a revolt against the colonial rulers.

On November 23, 1929, an organized riot spread throughout eastern Nigeria, starting from Calabar and going all the way to Owerri. Women stormed British administrative offices, blocked roads, attacked courthouses, and released prisoners from jails. They attacked European-owned business such as banks and department stores. They chanted songs known culturally as "sitting on men" as a way to subdue men into surrendering.

While the women did not harm anyone, they caused enough rioting to cause the colonial administration to send in police and armed military to quell the uprising. The British soldiers shot into the crowd of protesting women, killing many of them, and they burned down villages as punishment for the men who stood aside and did nothing to stop the rioting. The number of women who participated in this uprising has been estimated to be anywhere between 15,000 and 25,000.[27]

These women remained defiant despite the military attack and slaughter. They sat outside the various district colonial administrative offices for days until the colonial administration gave them a written assurance that they were not going to be taxed. Some of the corrupt warrant chiefs were also made to vacate their positions for the sake of peace. The effects of this concession have remained in Nigeria until today. While any able-bodied man could be stopped at any intersection by the internal revenue workers and asked to show proof of tax payment, no woman would be stopped and asked to show the same evidence. Women in Nigeria still do not pay taxes unless they are employed in a setting where taxes can be deducted from their paychecks. Market women still do not pay head taxes in the year 2019, as this book is being written.

One would expect that this victory over taxation would translate into victory in other spheres of life, but progress for Nigerian women, while steady, has been slow. Those women who have access to education fare much better than their counterparts with little or no education. While Nigerian women are competing healthily with their male counterparts in academic achievements, they have remained less represented in fields such as engineering and technology.

Women have made significant advances in the field of medical science in Nigeria, with a good number of Nigerian women employed as medical doctors. Nigerian women are represented in the armed forces, in the navy, police, immigration, and other parts of the armed forces. They are also making advances in business, though big business still remains men's turf. Again, most of these women hail from the Christian-dominated southern regions, unlike those from the Muslim north, where progress has been the slowest.

POVERTY AND WOMEN'S RIGHTS

Women are among the world's poorest people. The academic language used in discussing female poverty in relation to men in the past thirty years is the "feminization of poverty." This language is traced back to the groundbreaking work of Diane Pearce in 1978 titled, "The Feminization of Poverty: Women, Work and Welfare."[28] In this article, Pearce argued that poverty was rapidly becoming a women's problem. She stated that in 1976, two out of every three of the fifteen million poor people in the United States were women.

When you look at magazines, television, and newspapers, the faces of poverty you see are mostly the faces of women and their children. Studies continue to show that there is a high proportion of female-headed households in poverty across the world. The fact that in many parts of the world, women more than men face many restrictions on their choices and opportunities often results in lower income for women. The fact that women do not enjoy equal opportunities with men in education, employment, and other life opportunities translates to limited income and a greater likelihood of poverty.[29]

As mentioned earlier, an article on closing the gender gap in mobile technology reveals that while the ownership of mobile phones has skyrocketed worldwide, a woman's chance of owning a mobile phone is still 21 percent less than that of a man's.[30] This percentage climbs even higher if that woman lives in Africa, South Asia, or the Middle East.[31] A study by Hanna Jokinen-Gordon (2012) reveals that research has consistently found that even in the United States, later-life poverty is concentrated more highly among women than among men. Factors responsible for this have been traced to a combination of forces from early childbirths to disadvantaged social contexts, divorce or singleness, and many other factors. These factors seem to impact the economic well-being of women in significant ways.

An editorial article from the *American Journal of Public Health* indicates that life expectancy has declined among low-educated women in the United States. The editorial points out that between 1990 and 2000, life expectancy among white women with zero to less than twelve years of schooling declined by one year, but increased by one year among those with thirteen or more years of education. Socioeconomic resources such as education, employment and income are considered the primary factors that shape longevity.[32]

Where these resources are not accessible to women, due to traditional or cultural inhibitions, gender discrimination, or political- or policy-related reasons, the life expectancy of those women is reduced as a consequence. Data shows that traditionally female jobs pay much less to women than they pay to men. Table 4.2 shows the disparities that exist.

Table 4.2. Median Hourly Wage of Women and Men in Traditionally Female Jobs

	Women's median weekly earnings	Women's earnings as a percent of men's	Men's median weekly earnings	Share of female workers in occupation (percent)	Share of male workers in occupation as percent of all male workers	Share of female workers in occupation as percent of all female workers
All Full-time Workers	$770	81.8%	$941	44.4%	100% (62,980,00)	100% (50,291,000)
20 Most Common Occupations for Women						
Registered nurses	$1,143	90.7%	$1,260	88.8%	0.4%	4.5%
Elementary and middle school teachers	$987	86.7%	$1,139	78.4%	1.0%	4.4%
Secretaries and administrative assistants	$735	86.3%	$852	94.5%	0.2%	4.1%
Customer service representatives	$637	89.5%	$712	65.6%	1.0%	2.5%
Nursing, psychiatric, and home health aides	$493	84.6%	$583	88.2%	0.3%	2.4%
Managers, all other	$1,251	76.8%	$1,629	38.7%	2.9%	2.3%
First-line supervisors of retail sales workers	$639	71.7%	$891	42.4%	2.2%	2.0%
Cashiers	$422	85.6%	$493	72.2%	0.6%	2.0%
Accountants and auditors	$1,065	76.7%	$1,389	58.9%	1.0%	1.8%
First-line supervisors of office and administrative support workers	$819	83.0%	$987	67.7%	0.6%	1.7%
Receptionists and information clerks	$599	91.9%	$652	92.6%	0.1%	1.6%
Office clerks, general	$670	85.9%	$780	84.8%	0.2%	1.6%
Retail salespersons	$523	74.3%	$704	38.8%	1.8%	1.5%
Maids and housekeeping cleaners	$439	86.4%	$508	84.3%	0.2%	1.4%
Bookkeeping, accounting, and auditing clerks	$716	96.4%	$743	87.0%	0.1%	1.2%
Financial managers	$1,222	71.1%	$1,719	55.0%	0.8%	1.2%
Personal care aides	$479	92.1%	$520	82.7%	0.2%	1.2%
Waiters and waitresses	$475	89.1%	$533	65.0%	0.5%	1.2%
Social workers	$900	96.3%	$935	82.8%	0.2%	1.2%
Secondary school teachers	$1,091	89.0%	$1,226	57.1%	0.6%	1.0%
Percent of all men and women					15.1%	40.7%

The poverty rate among single female heads of household in the United States rose between 2000 and 2013, from 25.4 percent to 31.6 percent. Most of these women were single mothers with limited education, limited skills, and fewer employment prospects.[33] With the growth of childbearing outside of marriage, higher divorce rate, and persistent gender inequality, American women will continue to be more disproportionately poor than men, especially with a growing longer life span than US men. Added to this is the fact that the proportion of children who are living with single mothers has risen steadily, making poverty in homes with female heads of household even more staggering.[34]

An interesting study from the United Kingdom reveals that while the gender gap in poverty is shrinking, women remain the more impacted by poverty than men. Analysis of the effects of the 2008–2009 recession in the UK, with the government austerity programs and reform that followed, show that they have had more of an impact on women than men. A study by Rubery and Rafferty (2013) indicates that women fared much worse than men between 2007 and 2011.[35]

Demot and Pantgazis (2014) show that of the 308,000 public sector jobs lost in the UK between 2010 and 2012, they were predominantly women's jobs, with female unemployment rising by 61,000 between 2011 and 2013. In 2012, the women living in Britain were poorer and more deprived than men, across all measures used in their study. While the gaps might not be as significant as they were in the past, women still remain the less fortunate.[36]

Another study from Sweden (Trygeed & Kareholt, 2014) linked female victims of severe violence to poverty. It indicated that women who were exposed to severe violence were mostly exposed to poorer financial situations before their assault. These women often suffered the violence at the hands of domestic partners or someone they knew. The study further revealed that being young, unemployed, divorced, or single with children increased the chances of a women becoming a victim of severe violence. These women had limited assets in terms of education and economic resources, and they tended to become dependent on those who assaulted them.[37]

Two studies done in the 1990s, one by the European Community Household Panel and a survey on income and living conditions, revealed a gap between men and women in Spain. While the magnitude of the gap might not be as alarming as in other countries, the collected data showed persistent poverty among women more than men. Subsequent data from 1996 to 2001 and from 2004 to 2010 also showed a higher poverty rate among women than men. They revealed a higher risk of poverty among unemployed married women as well as single women who were working full time. The study showed higher poverty rates in women who were over the age of sixty-five as well as widows who depended on retirement pensions.[38]

A study on the multidimensional measurement of poverty among women in Africa studied fourteen countries in sub-Saharan Africa. The study found three subgroups of countries in sub-Saharan Africa. The first subgroup had 50 percent of the women in those countries living in poverty, the second had between 30 and 50 percent of the women in the countries living in poverty, and the third had less than 30 percent of the women in those countries living in poverty. The study showed that poverty was higher in rural areas of sub-Saharan Africa than in urban areas, and that lack of education is the highest contributor to female poverty rates, with deprivations in empowerment as the second causative factor.[39]

Another study focused on female trafficking in Nigeria. This study revealed a startling number of Nigerian girls and women who are trafficked to Europe and the United States as sex slaves or into domestic servitude. Some of these girls were trafficked voluntarily due to such prevailing factors as poverty and unemployment, among many other factors. Beyond poverty, many of these girls leave home excited about potential opportunities overseas, unaware of the dangerous fate that awaits them in Europe, the United States, and some Arab nations.

These girls and women arrive in these countries to face the violence of sexual abuse and physical assaults. The study blames a combination of forces of poverty, illiteracy, unemployment, and poor living conditions, coupled with government failures to enforce meaningful economic reforms as factors responsible for the migration of these women away from home.[40]

A study on the poverty among female heads of household in Jeddah City in Saudi Arabia (Fadaak, 2010) revealed that even in a prosperous nation like Saudi Arabia, female poverty remains a concern. Saudi Arabia does not have an official poverty line, and the state provides its citizens with free education and health care. If citizens cannot support themselves, their families are expected to support them or charity agencies come to their rescue.

The study reveals that within the Mecca province, females and female household heads represent 56.5 percent of the poor in that province, with about 36,896 single women and female heads of household. In Jeddah City, the number of poor people who received income support in 2007 was 35,639. Female heads of household made up 70 percent of the poor people in Jeddah City.[41]

A similar study focused on caretaker women in Iran. Caretaker women are defined to include those women who provide the primary care of their households due to factors such as divorce, widowhood, husband's disability or incarceration, unemployment, or drug addiction. The study focused on those women who were receiving support from an organization known as Behzisti. By the end of 2009, this organization supported 5,031 women. Among these women, 2,317 were classified as illiterate, with 1,140 having an elementary education, 161 having a high school education, 499 with a diploma, 43 enrolled in the university, and 85 with a university education or higher.

The study identified eight factors that have led to a culture of poverty among these women in Iran: irresponsibility, disparticipation, secrecy, gender bias, low-risking, beggary, forced remarriage, and sexual vulnerability.[42] The point in referencing this study, however, is the high percentage of illiterate women who are poor.

In China, since the 1995 World Conference on Women in Beijing, China has taken steps to address women's issues. However, China's poverty alleviation programs have not paid any specific attention to women; rather, China focuses on the "person." A survey conducted by All China National Women's Federation and the National Bureau of Statistics between 1990 and 2000 reveals that while women's income has seen impressive increases, the disparity between men's and women's income remains high.

In 1999, women earned only 59.6 percent of men's earnings among those employed in agriculture, forestry, animal husbandry, and fishing. That same year, there were 19.3 percent more women in poverty in China than men.[43] This study further reveals that educationally, there are 156 men in undergraduate education for every 100 females, and 909 men in graduate schools for every 100 females. This disparity in educational opportunities indicates that the poverty gap will continue to be wide between men and women in China.

A 2013–2014 economic survey of Pakistan revealed that 61 percent of Pakistanis live under the poverty line, with less than $2-a-day income. Women are said to be more likely to be poorer than men, and they face discrimination on access to education, health care, and other resources. Female workers tend to make less money than men, and they end up saving less than men, and are thus unable to meet emergency needs when they arrive. Female workers are expected to obtain male permission to leave their homes, and they often depend on middlemen for doing things in the public. This limits their ability to be socially engaged and to access public resources.[44]

GLOBAL MOVEMENTS TOWARD GENDER EQUITY

The first International Women's Day was celebrated March 8, 1911. This day was marked by rallies and campaigns on the rights of women to education, work, and hold public office; and rallies were also held to end discrimination against women. When this day was marked a hundred years later in 2011, data showed that in the UK, a 17 percent pay gap still existed between men and women.[45] In this section, we will examine the various global movements toward gender equity that have made a significant impact on the rights of women since 1911. The United Nations, since World War II, has been the primary agency championing women's right issues on a global level. Some of the movements we will examine here fall under UN conventions and declarations.

Convention on the Political Rights of Women, 1953

This convention, which came on the heels of World War II, was convened in recognition of the continuing problem of gender inequity and the disenfranchisement of women in various countries of the world. The preamble of this declaration states that the desire of the contracting nations was to see the implementation of the principles of equality of rights for both men and women as contained in the UN Charter.

The consenting parties agreed that women should be entitled to vote and be voted for in all elections. They agreed that in keeping with national laws, they are entitled to be considered on equal terms with men without discrimination. They consented that women should be entitled to hold public offices, and to exercise public functions on equal terms with men without discrimination.[46]

Convention on the Nationality of Married Women, 1957

This convention addressed situations in which women lost their citizenship as a result of marriage. The convention adopted that in recognition of Article 15 of the Universal Declaration of Human Rights of the United Nations General Assembly, every individual has the right to nationality, that no one should be arbitrarily deprived of the right to keep or change nationality, and that such rights should be exercised without distinction of sex.

The contracting states agreed that neither the contracting nor the dissolution of marriage should affect a woman's nationality. It also prevented a wife from losing her nationality based on the acquisition or renunciation of nationality by her husband. It allowed alien wives to acquire their husband's nationality upon their request.[47]

Convention on Consent to Marriage, Minimum Age for Marriage, and Registration of Marriages, 1962

This convention, which opened for signatures and ratification to consenting nations on November 7, 1962, was enforced December 9, 1964. The declaration stated that the objective was to promote universal respect for, and observance of, human rights, as well as all fundamental freedoms that apply to humans without the distinctions of race, sex, language, or religion. Appealing to Article 16 of the Universal Declaration of Human Rights that men and women of full age are entitled to equal rights pertaining to marriage, during the contracting and dissolution of marriage; that marriage shall be entered into only with the free and full consent of the individuals involved.

In keeping with these principles, the convention agreed that no marriage could be legally entered into without the full and free consent of both parties. Such consent was to be expressed in person, publicly, and in the presence of witnesses and an official competent to solemnize the marriage. It agreed that states should legislate a minimum age for marriage, and that no marriage should be entered into by anyone underage, except where the competent authority has granted a dispensation regarding age in the interest of the intending spouses. It required all marriages to be registered in an appropriate official registry.[48]

This convention aimed at addressing the complex issues of early marriage of girls, which stood in their way to a good education in many societies. It aimed at addressing arranged and forced marriages, which often were damaging to girls and their futures. It aimed at granting girls measurable rights to choose their own marriage partners, when to get married, and how to get married.

World Conference of the International Year of Women, 1975

The World Conference of the International Year of Women was held in Mexico City from June 19 to July 2, 1975. At this conference, the consenting nations agreed that underdevelopment in countries imposed a double burden of exploitation on women, and that there was an urgency toward improving the status of women and in finding more and effective opportunities for them to access the same opportunities that abounded for men, and for them to actively participate in the development of their countries and contribute to world peace.

They adopted a number of principles for gender equity, among which were the following:

- Equality between men and women means equality in their dignity and worth as persons, as well equality in rights, opportunities, and responsibilities.
- To ensure full integration into national development and participation in securing and maintaining international peace, all obstacles that stand in the way of women enjoying equal status must be eliminated.
- Equality between men and women should be guaranteed in the family, and men should more actively share in the responsibilities of the family life so

as to enable the women to become more actively involved in the life and activities of their communities.
- Women's right to work, to receive equal pay as men, and to be valued and provided with conditions for advancement at work were strongly reaffirmed.[49]

The convention affirmed the rights of women to decide for themselves on matters pertaining to the marriage contract. They called the underutilization of the potential of about half the world's population toward contributing to social and economic development a serious obstacle to global development. The participating nations were given ten years (from 1975 to 1985) to demonstrate long-term effort toward the achievement of the set objectives of the convention (United Nations, 1975).[50]

UN Decade for Women

The United Nations, in consideration of the 1975 World Conference of the International Year of Women, along with its declaration on the rights of women and future actions for the advancement of women's rights, declared the years from 1976 to 1985 as the United Nations Decade for Women. The goal was equality, development, and peace with sustained national and international actions. In this declaration, the United Nations urged governments around the world to take measures to ensure equal and effective participation of women in the political, economic, social, and cultural lives of their societies at regional, national, and international levels. It called upon financial institutions to give priority to financing development of projects that would promote the integration of women into the development of their communities.[51] It is clear that women and development were the primary focus for the Decade of Women.

Convention on the Elimination of All Forms of Discrimination against Women, 1979

The United Nations' General Assembly declaration from this assembly is often referred to as International Bill of Rights for Women. Concerned that discrimination against women had persisted despite various previous attempts by the UN, this convention articulated thirty articles that clearly defined discrimination against women. They also put together an agenda for national actions aimed at ending discrimination against women.

They defined discrimination against women as "any distinction, exclusion or restriction made on the basis of sex which has the effect or purpose of impairing or nullifying the recognition, enjoyment or exercise by women, irrespective of their marital status, on a basis of equality of men and women, of human rights and fundamental freedoms in the political, economic, social, cultural, civil or any other field."[52]

The convention required all consenting nations to adopt legislations, sanctions, and all other appropriate measures to protect the rights of women, to eliminate discrimination against women by individuals and organizations, and to repeal national penal provisions that constitute discrimination against women. It required consenting states to afford women equal rights as men under the law.[53]

Article 2 of the Convention called on all consenting states to take all appropriate measures to modify or abolish all existing laws, regulations, customs, and practices that constituted discrimination against women. Article 5 (a) called for them to use all appropriate measures to modify social and cultural patterns of conduct of both men and women to ensure the elimination of prejudices and practices that were based on the ideas of the inferiority of women or the superiority of men.[54]

Declaration on the Elimination of Violence against Women, 1993

The declaration of this convention recognized what it called the urgent need for the universal application to women of the rights and principles with regard to the equality, security, liberty, integrity, and dignity of all humans. It noted that those rights and principles are enshrined in international instruments, including the Universal Declaration of Human Rights, the International Covenant on Civil and Political Rights, the International Covenant on Economic, Social and Cultural Rights, the Convention on the Elimination of All Forms of Discrimination against Women, and the Convention against Torture and other Cruel Inhuman or Degrading Treatment or Punishment.

Against this backdrop, it defined violence against women as "any act of gender-based violence that results in, or is likely to result in, physical, sexual or psychological harm or suffering to women, including threats of such acts, coercion or arbitrary deprivation of liberty, whether occurring in public or in private life."[55]

Fourth World Conference on Women, Beijing China—Beijing Declaration, 1995

The goal of the Beijing conference, otherwise known as the United Nations Fourth World Conference on Women, was to explore strategies for the advancement of women, and to remove all obstacles that have stood in the way of women attaining active participation in all spheres of public and private life. This conference established that equality between men and women is a matter of human rights and that it is a condition for social justice and a fundamental prerequisite for development and peace in the world.

It called for a sustained and long-term commitment to the advancement of women's rights and emphasized that a shared common concern on women's rights between men and women was necessary to attain gender equity around the world. The conference called for immediate and concerted action of all toward the creation of a peaceful, just, and humane world that is based on freedoms, human rights, and social justice.[56]

This conference is built on many other conferences and conventions we have already addressed, and those that we have not been able to mention here due to limited space (e.g., the Nairobi Conference and the Geneva Declaration for Rural Women). The outcomes and goals of this conference were revisited every five years (in 2000, 2005, 2010, and 2015). The question that still remains is why these international conferences and the level of attention they give to women's rights issues have not changed things more drastically.

VIOLENCE AGAINST WOMEN: A GLOBAL CONCERN

The final area to be addressed, though not the only remaining area of concern, is the area of violence against women. Violence against women occurs in various forms, but for the purposes of this chapter, we will limit our discussion to domestic violence, sexual assaults and harassment, and war crimes against women.

The United Nations defined violence against women as any act of violence that is gender-based and results in or is likely to result in physical, sexual, or mental harm or suffering of a woman. It includes threats of acts of violence, coercion, and arbitrary deprivation of liberty, whether in public or private life.[57] The World Health Organization has identified violence against women as a public health problem that has affected women all over the world.

Data from population-based studies show that 35 percent of women worldwide have experienced physical and/or sexual violence from either an intimate partner or a non-partner or both in their lifetime. The same reports indicate that an average of 30 percent of women who have been in an intimate relationship have reported physical or sexual violence by their partners. As many as 38 percent of murders of women are committed by their intimate partners. Fifteen percent of women in Japan and 71 percent of women in Ethiopia reported physical and/or sexual violence from their partners in 2005.

Forty-two percent of women who experience intimate partner violence do report injury as a result of the violence.

Some of the risk factors that expose women to violence as identified by the World Health Organization include lower levels of education, exposure to child maltreatment, harmful use of alcohol, having multiple partners, attitudes that are accepting or tolerant of violence and gender inequality, and marital discord and/or dissatisfaction.[58] See the WHO data in Figure 4.2 on violence from intimate and non-intimate partners in 2010.

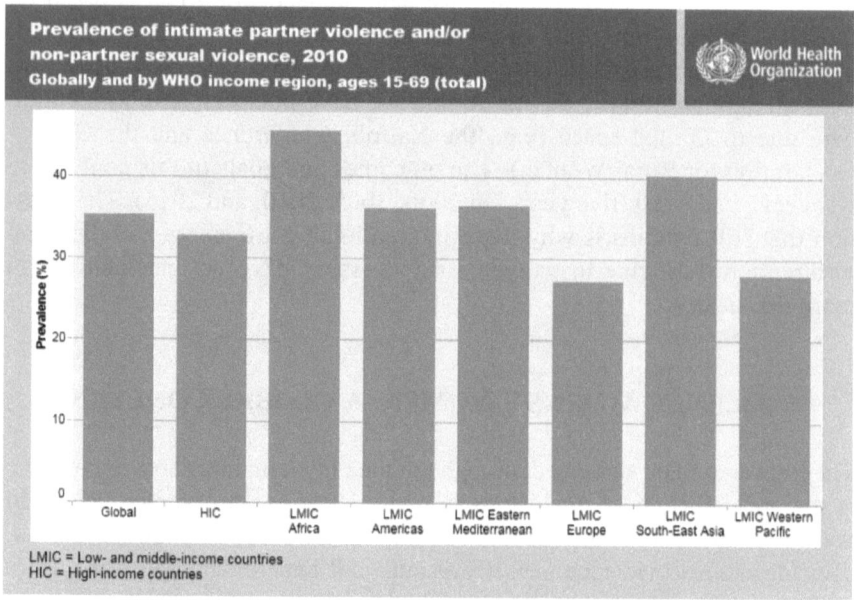

Figure 4.2. WHO Data on Violence against Women from Intimate and Non-Intimate Partners

In the United States, elder abuse, which is the mistreatment of persons of ages sixty and above, is more rampant among older women than men. In the state of Illinois, for example, a report from the public health department indicates that three out of every four elder abuse cases have females as the victims. Forty-seven percent of such abuse cases come from adult children of these elderly people, 19 percent from their spouses, 9 percent from other relatives, and 9 percent from grandchildren.[59]

On the specific topic of sexual assault and harassment, first let's define sexual harassment as unwanted and unwelcome sexual advance or contact. In the United States, a 1992 Supreme Court ruling, *Franklin v. Gwinnett County Public School*, held that sexual harassment violates Title IX and was sufficient ground for students to seek monetary damages when the harassment came from a teacher.

Another Supreme Court ruling, *Davis v. Monroe County Board of Education* of 1999, ruled that schools may also be liable under Title IX if a student harasses another student sexually to the knowledge and deliberate indifference of the school authorities.[60] A US Department of Justice report on sexual assaults indicates that one in every six women in the United States has been a victim of attempted or completed sexual assault, and 41.4 percent of women who were raped also reported physical assault during the rape.

The US Census Bureau estimates that one million women are stalked every year, and that 12.6 million women are stalked in their lifetimes.[61] Girls between the ages of sixteen and nineteen are four times more likely to be rape victims than the general population. Eighty-two percent of all juvenile rape victims are female. One out of nine girls is sexually assaulted or abused by an adult. In the year 2012 alone, 346,830 women were raped, with an estimated 17,342 pregnancies resulting from those rapes.[62] In the United States military, 5 percent of all active-duty women were reportedly exposed to unwanted sexual contact in 2013. Nearly half of the assaults reported by women in the military were penetrative assaults (which includes rape and penetration with an object). Sadly, the incidents of sexual assaults in the military are increasing instead of decreasing.

In 2013, the total reported incidents of sexual assault were 5,539, but in 2014 that figure rose to 6,236.[63] It is clear, therefore, that sexual assault against women remains an area needing attention in the battle for gender equity. In fact, there is a rape-blind culture that encourages bad behavior for men and discourages abused women from coming forward. Those kinds of cultures must be confronted and altered for good.

Finally, women and children tend to suffer more violence than men in war-torn areas of the world. Data on rape statistics in wars tends to be hard to gather, but one report indicates that in the Bosnia War, between 14,000 to 50,000 women and girls were raped, while estimates range between 15,700 to a half million girls and women who were raped in the Rwandan war. Due to a breakdown in law and order in conflict zones, sexual and physical violence against women tends to escalate and go on unbridled.[64] Girls and women are often taken captives as sex slaves and domestic help without their having any recourse.

In April 2014, 276 high school girls were kidnapped by a terrorist group, Boko Haram, from Chibok in northeastern Nigeria. These girls have been held as sex and domestic slaves for years now. When, in 2015, some of them were rescued by the joint forces of the African Union, most of them came home pregnant. Even in the year 2019, girls and women continue to face more dangers of physical and sexual assaults than men. This is a continuing area of concern, especially given the fact that data on sexual assaults and rape in conflict zones were not collected until just recently.[65]

Chapter Five

The Advancement of Gender Equity in the United States

CHAPTER OBJECTIVES

The goal of this chapter is to discuss important movements, legal cases, and policies that have advanced gender equity in the United States over the years. The topics discussed here are only representative samples, as there is not sufficient room to discuss all movements, laws, and policies in detail. The goal is to provide the reader with a cursory historical outline of the women's rights movement in the United States as it has been advanced through the years, and to highlight organizations that individual educators may join and work through if they desire to become more actively involved in the advancement of women's rights in the United States.

INTRODUCTION

Women's rights movement in the United States, like other human rights issues, have been possible only as a result of strenuous push and shove both ideologically and practically. The history of women's rights in the United States is a history of slow and painful crumbling of ironclad walls that restricted the rights of women and made them second-class citizens. The fact, however, that society restricted women's rights and opportunities does not mean that women generally settled with the assigned roles and accepted them. Through every generation, from the earliest days of the colonies, women challenged the system and questioned the assumptions underlying the restrictions imposed on them. In the book *An Introduction to Multicultural Education: From Theory to Practice* (2010), a detailed portrait of female activists is given, of those who championed the course of gender rights beginning from Ann Hutchinson in the early days of the New England colonies to Hillary Rodham Clinton, whose unsuccessful bid for the US presidency has left a lasting impact. There is no need to repeat those discussions in this book; rather, we look at some of the movements and legal/legislative actions that have helped to advance women's rights over the years.

THE NATIONAL LEAGUE OF WOMEN VOTERS

Founded during the Convention of the National American Suffrage Association in 1920, this organization came into life just six months before the ratification of the Nineteenth Amendment to the US Constitution, which gave women the right to vote. The League helped the many American women (numbering up to twenty million) to effectively carry out their new responsibility as voters.

The organization emerged as a grassroots movement with no partisan agenda. It was a group committed to advocacy on matters pertaining to women, and it engaged in addressing issues that concerned the general public. Important names such as Eleanor Roosevelt helped to shape the direction of this organization.[1] In recent years, the League has continued to make lasting contributions, such as the role it played in passing the Help America Vote Act of 2002, the Bipartisan Campaign Finance Reform Act of 2002, and its ongoing engagement in active voter education campaign even today.[2]

THE NATIONAL COUNCIL OF NEGRO WOMEN (NCNW)

The National Council of Negro Women was founded by Mary McLeod Bethune in 1935. She was serving as the advisor on minority affairs to President Franklin Delano Roosevelt. McLeod Bethune's passion was a desire to unleash the potential of women through a national movement. She saw her organization as "a national organization of national organizations," with the goal of bringing women's organizations together to promote development and peace.

Twenty-eight women leaders from across the nation responded to her initial call, and she envisioned the movement to function as a clearinghouse that facilitated networking and the building of coalitions for advocacy and activism on issues pertaining to women, their communities, and their families.[3] Among the many accomplishments of the group is the promoting of equality among black women.

THE EQUAL PAY ACT OF 1963

The history of this act traces back to the Fair Labor Standards Act of 1938. It was amended from its original form and handed over to the Equal Employment Opportunities Commission (EEOC) for administration and enforcement. This act, which took effect under President John F. Kennedy, prohibits discrimination against women on wages when those women are employed under the same establishment to perform jobs requiring the same skills, efforts, and responsibilities as men.

The specifics of this law are as follows:

(1) No employer having employees subject to any provisions of this section shall discriminate, within any establishment in which such employees are employed, between employees on the basis of sex by paying wages to employees in such establishment at a rate less than the rate at which he pays wages to employees of the opposite sex in such establishment for equal work on jobs the performance of which requires equal skill, effort, and responsibility, and which are performed under similar working conditions, except where such payment is made pursuant to (i) a seniority system; (ii) a merit system; (iii) a system which measures earnings by quantity or quality of production; or (iv) a differential based on any other factor other than sex: Provided, That an employer who is paying a wage rate differential in violation of this subsection shall not, in order to comply with the provisions of this subsection, reduce the wage rate of any employee.

(2) No labor organization, or its agents, representing employees of an employer having employees subject to any provisions of this section shall cause or attempt to cause such an employer to discriminate against an employee in violation of paragraph (1) of this subsection.

(3) For purposes of administration and enforcement, any amounts owing to any employee which have been withheld in violation of this subsection shall be deemed to be unpaid minimum wages or unpaid overtime compensation under this chapter.

(4) As used in this subsection, the term "labor organization" means any organization of any kind, or any agency or employee representation committee or plan, in which employees participate and which exists for the purpose, in whole or in part, of dealing with employers concerning grievances, labor disputes, wages, rates of pay, hours of employment, or conditions of work.[4]

The enactment of this law was done in recognition of the fact that corporations that discriminate against women in wage payment depress the wages and living conditions of those workers, adversely affecting their quality of life as well as their health and efficiency. They also prevent a maximum utilization of available labor resources (EEOC).

TITLE VII OF THE CIVIL RIGHTS ACT OF 1964

This law prohibits discrimination in employment on the basis of race, color, religion, sex, and national origin. It is defined as an act *"to enforce the constitutional right to vote, to confer jurisdiction, upon the district courts of the United States to provide injunctive relief against discrimination in public accommodations, to authorize the Attorney General to institute suits to protect constitutional rights in public facilities and public education, to extend the Commission on Civil Rights, to prevent discrimination in federally assisted programs, to establish a Commission on Equal Employment Opportunity, and for other purposes."*[5]

This law made it illegal for employers to discriminate against anyone on the basis of religion, race, color of skin, sex, or national origin. Labor organizations could not exclude anyone from membership on the basis of these factors. This law led to the creation of the Equal Employment Opportunity Commission, made up of five members appointed by the president. This law, more than any before it, made women's rights in America a civil rights issue. It is important, however, to note that the inclusion of gender protection in this law was not part of the original goal of this law.

The law was focused exclusively on civil rights along racial and nationality lines, but a Southern congressman by name of Howard Smith, seeking to kill the entire civil rights bill, added the gender element with hopes that it would help to kill the bill. A number of women in the Congress seized the opportunity and pushed for the passage of the law, thereby handing civil rights and gender rights activists a double win.[6] The significance of this law lies in the fact that it afforded African Americans, women, and other minority people certain citizenship rights that had been deprived them for centuries. Dr. Martin Luther King Jr. described it as a "second emancipation" (A&E Television Networks, 2018). Other civil rights laws, such as the Voting Rights Act of 1965 and the Fair Housing Act of 1968, were all by-products of this groundbreaking law.

This law was amended in 2009 with the addition of the Lily Ledbetter Fair Pay Act of 2009. Even the setting up and commissioning of the Equal Employment Opportunity Commission is not without its limitations. The Commission was established with practically no power and no personnel. As of 1966, it had only thirty investigators serving the entire nation, with no real authority to prosecute anyone who violated the law. It was practically set up to investigate and engage in conciliatory talks with anyone who violated the laws, without any judicial power to prosecute them. Over the years, much has changed, however, and it has become a more powerful agency helping to advance the rights of minorities and women across the nation.

On October 6, 2015, Governor Jerry Brown of California signed into law what has been called the strongest law in favor of equal pay for women in the nation, the California SB 358. Among other things, this law requires employers to prove specific skill sets or seniority when paying different wages to men and women. It also provides protections for women to speak up and discuss fair wages with their colleagues and employers.

THE NATIONAL ORGANIZATIONS FOR WOMEN

The National Organization for Women (NOW) is an activist organization that was founded in 1966 with the goal of promoting equal rights for women. It was founded by a group of feminists whose goal was to challenge sex discrimination in all the various areas of American life where it was showing up, but with a special focus on employment.[7] The organization's purpose focused on women's rights as equal partners with men, and their activism focused on confronting gender inequality with concrete actions, with the goal of helping women develop their fullest potential. They stated their commitment as "equality, freedom, and dignity for women."

The organization wanted to put women into the mainstream of American political, economic, and social life. Some of the key issues they addressed included employment, education, marriage, divorce, and gender roles. It was originally constituted by twenty-eight women in a hotel room in Washington, DC. Betty Friedan was elected its first president.[8] The organization in its current form is comprised of both men and women, and it is said to have had a membership of about 250,000 around the turn of the century.[9] As of the year 2006, the membership was at 500,000.[10]

THE NATIONAL WOMEN'S POLITICAL CAUCUS

Formed in 1971 with the primary goal of identifying, recruiting, training, endorsing, and supporting women who desire to seek political office, the National Women's Political Caucus is a nonpartisan political organization. It helps women run successful political campaigns by offering fund-raising support, developing a political platform, recruiting and motivating volunteers, and helping candidates secure media coverage. The organization has also lobbied successfully to get women appointed into public offices and other important policy-making positions.[11]

TITLE IX OF THE EDUCATIONAL AMENDMENTS OF 1972

The origin of Title IX goes back to the Civil Rights Act of 1964. Title IX itself was an education amendment to the Civil Rights Act. It could be seen as the final product of a series of actions and executive orders that followed the Civil Rights Act. In 1965, President Lyndon B. Johnson issued Executive Order 11246, which prohibited federal contractors from discriminating against individuals in relation to employment on the basis of race, color, religion, or national origin. This order was further amended in 1968 to include discrimination based on sex.

Title IX was passed by the US Congress into law on June 23, 1972, after about two years of strenuous work. The Act stated that, *"No person in the United States shall, on the basis of sex, be excluded from participation in, be denied the benefits of, or be subjected to discrimination under any education program or activity receiving Federal financial assistance."*[12] This would be the most sweeping and most far-reaching gender-based law in the United States. It has also remained the bedrock on which issues of gender equity in education have been based over the years.

Among the various provisions of this law were issues of equity in distribution of financial resources, equity in provisions to meet students' interests and abilities in athletics, providing equal athletic opportunities for both girls and boys, the prevention of sexual harassments in the classroom and in other educational settings, and in preventing discrimination against women on the basis of pregnancy, childbirth, or other reasons. Schools that receive federal funds must appoint a Title IX coordinator to oversee compliance to this law and to investigate any forms of sexual discrimination.

Valentin (1997) reports a fourfold increase of women in collegiate sports between 1972 and 1997, when she was writing. She provided the following data:

- In 1994, 63 percent of female high school graduates between the ages of sixteen and twenty-four enrolled in college, compared to 43 percent in 1973.
- In 1994, 27 percent of women earned bachelor's degrees, compared to 18 percent in 1971.
- In 1994, 38 percent of medical degrees awarded in the United States went to women, compared to 9 percent in 1972.
- In 1995, women made up 37 percent of college athletes in the United States, compared to 12 percent in 1972.
- In 1996, girls made up 39 percent of high school athletes, compared to 7.5 percent in 1971.
- In 1996, women won nineteen Olympic medals in the Summer Olympic Games, higher than any year previously.[13]

As of the year 2014, the Report Card on Gender Equity on College Sports reported the following on women in sports:

- The Grade for Head Coaches for all Division I Men's teams: 3.3 percent female.
- The Grade for Head Coaches for all Division I Women's teams: 38.2 percent female.
- The Grade for Head Coaches for all Division I Men's basketball teams: 0 percent female.
- The Grade for Head Coaches for all Division I Women's basketball teams: 59.2 percent female.[14]

The 2017 Annual reports on race- and gender-based hiring practices in college sports showed the following:

- A C-plus grade for racial hiring practices, with 78.3 points, a 0.2 point decrease from 78.5 points in the 2016 CSRGRC.
- A C-plus grade for gender hiring practices, with 75.1 points, up 2.5 points from 73.5 points in the 2016 CSRGRC (Lapchick, 2018).

While this shows progress in gender-related hiring practices, the progress remains slow.

THE NATIONAL ASSOCIATION OF WORKING WOMEN

The National Association of Working Women was formed in 1973 by a group of female office workers in the city of Boston who got fed up with feeling powerless and being underpaid and undervalued. They mobilized themselves with the goal of changing the way they were paid and how they were treated. They describe themselves today as one of the largest and most respected national membership organizations for working women in the United States.

This organization articulates its mission as building a movement for economic justice through the engagement of women toward improving their working conditions. Their goal includes protecting all women against workplace discrimination and sexual harassment, elevating women to the state of self-sufficiency and the ability to support their families, and working toward an economically just world where poverty and discrimination have been eliminated. Among the many things they claim as their victories and accomplishments are the Family and Medical Leave Act of 1993, the 1991 improvements in the US Civil Rights Act, the Pregnancy Discrimination Act, the Lily Ledbetter Fair Pay Act of 2009, and improved investments in child care and health care for working families.[15]

THE WOMEN'S EDUCATIONAL EQUITY ACT (WEEA)

The Women's Educational Equity Act (WEEA) was authorized into law by Public Law 93-380 of the Education Amendment of 1974. This law made provisions for educational equity for women and to assist educational institutions in meeting the requirements of the Title IX law. It also addressed issues of equity for women and girls who experienced multiple types of discrimination based on gender, race, ethnicity, or disability.

This law made available federal dollars in the form of grants for academic instruction, career counseling, and other support services for women and girls. Some of the specific activities covered under the law include the following:

- The development, evaluation, and dissemination of curricula, textbooks, and other educational material;
- Preservice and in-service training for educational personnel;
- Research, development, and other activities designed to advance educational equity;
- Guidance and counseling activities, including the development of bias-free tests;
- Educational activities to increase opportunities for adult women; and
- The expansion and improvement of educational programs and activities for women in vocational education, career education, physical education, and education administration.[16]

Other programs authorized under this law include school-to-work transition programs, the replication of exemplary gender equity programs, leadership training for girls and women, and programs and policies that address sexual harassment.[17] The goal of these programs was to compensate for years of deprivation and inequity that had targeted women and girls.

THE FEMINIST MAJORITY FOUNDATION

Founded in 1987, this movement articulated its goals as creating innovative, cutting-edge research, educational programs, and strategies that furthered women's equality and empowerment, while at the same time reducing violence against women. They aim at improving the economic and physical well-being of women and eliminating all forms of discrimination against women. Two important initiatives of this organization include the establishment of a National Clinic Defense Project, which aims at defending women's health clinics from anti-abortion activists, and to safeguard the constitutional rights of women to have an abortion.

The second initiative was the Campaign for RU-486 and Contraceptive Research. This campaign advocates for immediate access to RU-486 as a method for early abortion in the United States, and it calls for increased testing of drugs that have promise for treating meningioma, breast cancer, and other serious diseases. In recent years, they have released annual National Clinic Violence Surveys, showing how frequently abortion clinics are being targeted and attacked in the United States. They are involved in advocating gender equity on a number of fronts, including female representation in the police corps, battle against gender apartheid in Afghanistan, and many other gender equity causes.[18]

PROGRESS ON GENDER EQUITY IN THE UNITED STATES AND ACROSS THE GLOBE

It is necessary to highlight some "rays of sunshine" in gender equity issues. Women and the women's right movement in the United States have made significant progress on a number of fronts, and we will briefly highlight these areas of progress. As of the year 2014, women earned almost 60 percent of all undergraduate degrees, 60 percent of all master's degrees, 47 percent of all law degrees, and 48 percent of all medical degrees in the United States. They also earned more than 44 percent of all master's degrees in business and management, and they make up a significant percentage of the US labor force, with 59 percent of the college-educated, entry-level workforce being women.[19]

Since the passage of Title IX in the United States, girls' and women's participation in science, technology, engineering, and mathematics (STEM) has increased in a meaningful way. Most states in the United States now require two or more years of mathematics and science learning for high school graduation. This has given girls access to these fields in the same degree that boys have had it in high school. Data collected in 2000 showed that 65.7 percent of high school girls took chemistry, compared to 58 percent of high school boys. Girls reportedly outnumbered boys in precalculus, with boys slightly outnumbering girls in calculus. An increased number of girls are reportedly taking Advanced Placement (AP) classes in calculus and physics.

In 1970, women earned only 17.5 percent of bachelor degrees awarded in natural sciences and engineering, but by the year 2004, their percentage had risen to 38.4 percent, and by 2008 they were earning 50 percent of all degrees in the biological and agricultural sciences. Doctoral degrees earned by women in science and engineering rose from 6.7 percent in 1970 to 30.5 percent in 2008. As of 2008, women made up nearly 60 percent of all undergraduate students in US colleges. They made up about half of all master's, doctoral, law, and medical students as well.[20]

80   *Chapter Five*

In the area of employment, a 2013 data from the Bureau of Labor Statistics indicates that as of that year, women comprised of 57.2 percent of the labor force. There were 127.1 million working-age women in 2013, but only 72.7 million of them were in the labor force. Figure 5.1 shows the labor force participation across gender lines in 2013.

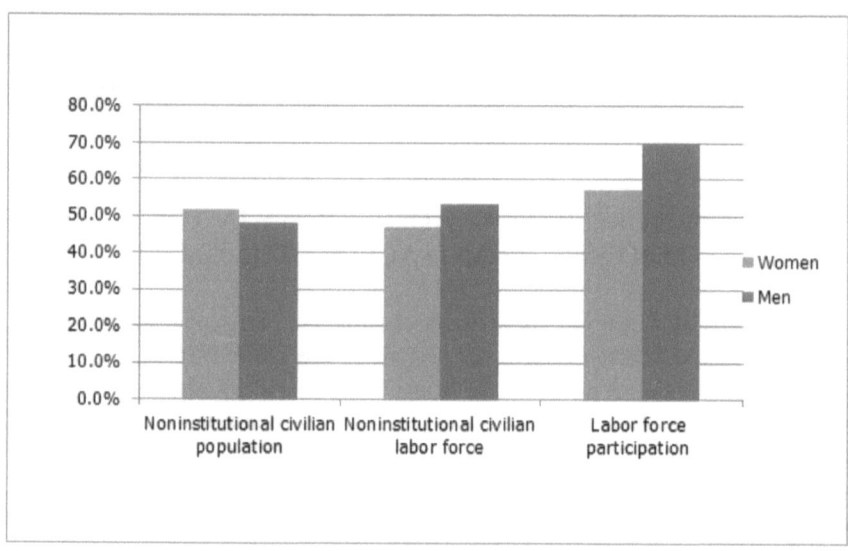

Figure 5.1.   2013 Labor Force Participation by Sex

While women's participation in the labor force is expected to continue to rise over the years, a 2022-year projection shows that labor force participation of women is expected to decline by 2022 to 46.8 percent from the 2013 number,[21] with 74 percent of employed women working full-time, while 24 percent work part-time. In the academy, there is a record increase in women's participation. Data from Title IX at 35 reflects the following for women employed in academic ranks in the colleges and universities (see Table 5.1).

Table 5.1.   Women Employment in the Academy

Status	1970	2005–06
Full Professors	8.7%	26.7%
Associate Professors	15.1%	40.5%
Assistant Professors	19.4%	47.5%
Instructors	32.5%	54.8%

In politics, the year 2012 was a significant landmark for gains in gender equity. Data shows that 40 percent of Americans by 2012 had at least one woman representing them in the US Senate. No US state could be considered a male-only legislature, and the US House of Representatives boasted twenty-eight women of color serving as representatives. A May 2013 poll showed that 90 percent of Americans would consider voting for a woman as president, with 51 percent convinced that women in the US Senate and House of Representatives were making a positive difference.[22] As of January 2019, Nancy Pelosi, the first female Speaker of the US House of Representatives, has earned a second term as the Democrats took over control of the House of Representatives. The freshman class of this new congress is remarkably made up of about 30 women in the House of Representatives, bringing the total number of women in the House to 102, the highest number of women ever in the history of the United States Congress.

CONTINUING AREAS OF CHALLENGE ON GENDER EQUITY IN THE UNITED STATES AND ACROSS THE WORLD

Despite the various areas of progress noted in the fight for gender equity, there remain many frontiers where the battle must continue to be waged. The educational front remains a battlefield, especially in the fields of science and technology. Women remain behind men in the number of degrees earned in the fields of science and technology.

In 2008, women earned only 29 percent of bachelor's degrees awarded in engineering and physics in the United States. They earned only 25.1 percent of all computer science degrees. Girls continue to be stigmatized and stereotyped with regard to their ability to engage in STEM courses. The culture of STEM courses and careers continues to isolate girls and women and provide little incentive to attract them into those fields.[23] While it can be said that women are making steady inroads into these otherwise male professions and occupations, the pace is too slow. This is more notably so when you look at the growing trend of female representation in the STEM fields, and the persistent underrepresentation of women in the STEM labor force.[24]

With regard to labor participation, while the population of women in the United States is slightly above that of men, women continue to be less represented in the labor force than men. Figure 5.2 shows the population and labor force participation between men and women in 2013.

Employment in the educational field is no better. While women have remained the dominant workforce in elementary and high school education, they still have far to go in employment in higher education. While women constitute 79 percent of the public school teachers in the United States, they make up only 44 percent of principals.

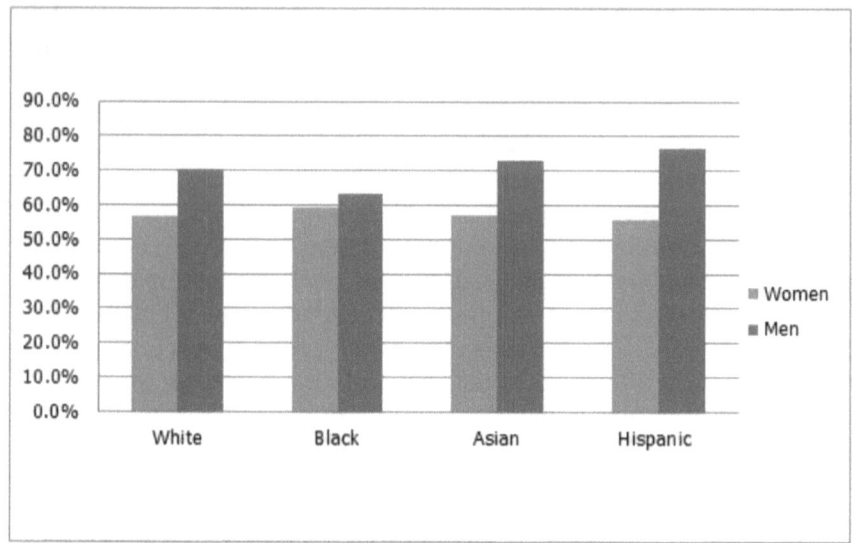

Figure 5.2. Population and Labor Force Participation by Sex, Race, and Ethnicity, 2013

In colleges and universities, women constitute 49 percent of part-time academic employees, but only 39 percent of full-time academic employees. The four industries with the highest percentage of women in 2013 were education and health care with 36.2 percent, wholesale and retail with 13.1 percent, professional and business services with 10.5 percent, and leisure and hospitality with 10.3 percent. The four with the lowest representation of women were mining, quarrying, and oil and gas extraction with 0.2 percent female, construction with 1.3 percent female, the information industry with 1.7 percent female, and transportation and utilities with 2.6 percent female.[25]

A second frontier is the area of pay equity. Women continue to earn less than men for the same amount of work, even in the year 2019. The US Census Bureau, the Bureau of Labor Statistics, and the US Department of Education all survey individuals, households, and businesses to collect information on people's salaries and earnings.

The pay gap is calculated by subtracting women's median earnings from men's median earnings and dividing the product with the men's median earning. The calculation is given as follows:

$$\text{Pay Gap} = \frac{[\text{Men's median earnings} - \text{Women's median earnings}]}{\text{Men's median earnings}}$$

A 2012 survey showed that the widest gap in a state-by-state study existed in the state of Wyoming, where women earned 64 percent of men's earnings, while the lowest gap was in Washington, DC, where women earned 90 percent of men's earnings. Despite the fact that studies have shown a major increase in female earnings since the 1970s, the gap in earning between males and females has peristed.[26]

In the field of education, while the pay gap has narrowed, women continue to earn 90 percent of male salaries in the K–12 educational setting. This gap is probably the smallest pay gap in all fields nationally, however. The gap is much higher when you transition into colleges and universities. Table 5.2 shows how this gap has narrowed in K–12 education since the year 2000, as well as the gap that has remained in pay equity in higher education.

Table 5.2. Percentage of Men's Pay Earned by Women Teachers

Occupation	2000	2001	2002	2003	2004	2005	2006
All Education, Training and Library occupations	75.1 (74.6)*	79.1 (74.0)	77.5 (74.2)	78.3 (73.8)	76.3 (73.4)	78.4 (73.8)	78.7 (74.2)
Elementary and middle School teachers	83.6 (82.0)	96.6 (81.1)	89.7 (81.6)	89.8 (81.7)	84.6 (81.3)	89.4 (82.2)	89.6 (82.2)
Secondary school teachers	87.6 (60.1)	89.4 (58.0)	92.0 (57.4)	91.3 (55.2)	86.3 (55.3)	89.3 (56.8)	93.7 (56.0)
Postsecondary teachers	79.8 (44.9)	76.7 (43.5)	77.6 (44.3)	79.0 (44.9)	76.2 (46.0)	78.8 (44.4)	74.5 (46.3)

In the general labor market, the gap has remained much wider. A gender income gap analysis study done of Australian workers showed that in 2013–2014, male employees earned $298 weekly more than female employees. In Canada, women earned 75.3 percent of men's weekly income in 2014. In the United States, women earned $0.78 for every $1.00 earned by men. This translates to men earning an average of $871 each week for women's $719, or put differently, $50,033 per year for women's $39,157.

US women in management and professional positions earn an average of $951 for men's $1,346.[27] Table 5.3 from the Institute for Women's Policy Research shows a trend over the years in the disparity between men's and women's wages.

Efforts under the Obama administration and his Democratic Congress to address pay equity issues and increase the minimum wage proved unsuccessful. Pay equity remains an area of concern not only in the United States, but in much of the developed world. The wage gap between men and women in Iceland as of 2010 was 13.0 percent, in Australia it was 14.0 percent, in France it was 14.0 percent, in Sweden it was 14.0 percent, in the United Kingdom it was 18.0 percent, in Switzerland it was 19.0 percent, in Germany it was 21.0 percent, in Israel it was 21.0 percent, and in Japan it was 29.0 percent.[28]

Table 5.3. Trend of Disparity between Men's and Women's Wages

Year	Median Annual Earnings, adjusted to 2014 dollars Full-time, Year Round Workers			Median Usual Weekly Earnings, adjusted to 2014 dollars Full-time, Wage and Salary Workers		
	Women	Men	Female to Male Earnings Ratio (%)	Women	Men	Female to Male Earnings Ratio (%)
1955			63.9%			
1960	$ 22,783	$ 37,549	60.7%			
1965	$ 25,157	$ 41,981	59.9%			
1970	$ 28,960	$ 48,780	59.4%			62.3
1975	$ 30,020	$ 51,040	58.8%			62.0
1980	$ 30,627	$ 50,909	60.2%	$ 575	$ 899	63.9%
1981	$ 29,972	$ 50,599	59.2%	$ 568	$ 883	64.3%
1982	$ 30,652	$ 49,643	61.7%	$ 584	$ 893	65.4%
1983	$ 31,433	$ 49,428	63.6%	$ 599	$ 898	66.7%
1984	$ 32,074	$ 50,385	63.7%	$ 602	$ 891	67.5%
1985	$ 32,780	$ 50,762	64.6%	$ 609	$ 893	68.2%
1986	$ 33,450	$ 52,047	64.3%	$ 626	$ 905	69.2%
1987	$ 33,710	$ 51,721	65.2%	$ 631	$ 904	69.8%
1988	$ 33,853	$ 51,255	66.1%	$ 630	$ 899	70.2%
1989	$ 34,597	$ 50,379	68.7%	$ 628	$ 895	70.1%
1990	$ 34,804	$ 48,597	71.6%	$ 627	$ 871	71.9%
1991	$ 34,838	$ 49,869	69.9%	$ 636	$ 857	74.2%
1992	$ 35,335	$ 49,919	70.8%	$ 641	$ 845	75.8%
1993	$ 35,083	$ 49,053	71.5%	$ 645	$ 836	77.3%
1994	$ 35,073	$ 48,734	72.0%	$ 637	$ 835	76.3%
1995	$ 34,699	$ 48,578	71.4%	$ 631	$ 836	75.5%
1996	$ 35,622	$ 48,292	73.8%	$ 631	$ 840	75.0%
1997	$ 36,725	$ 49,520	74.2%	$ 636	$ 853	74.6%
1998	$ 37,509	$ 51,262	73.2%	$ 664	$ 869	76.4%
1999	$ 37,388	$ 51,701	72.3%	$ 672	$ 880	76.4%
2000	$ 37,751	$ 51,208	73.7%	$ 678	$ 881	76.9%
2001	$ 39,064	$ 51,178	76.3%	$ 684	$ 896	76.4%
2002	$ 39,742	$ 51,883	76.6%	$ 696	$ 894	77.9%
2003	$ 39,545	$ 52,345	75.5%	$ 710	$ 894	79.4%
2004	$ 39,151	$ 51,127	76.6%	$ 718	$ 894	80.4%
2005	$ 38,631	$ 50,184	77.0%	$ 709	$ 875	81.0%
2006	$ 38,175	$ 49,618	76.9%	$ 705	$ 872	80.8%
2007	$ 40,076	$ 51,506	77.8%	$ 701	$ 875	80.2%
2008	$ 39,300	$ 50,979	77.1%	$ 702	$ 877	79.9%
2009	$ 40,038	$ 52,011	77.0%	$ 725	$ 904	80.2%
2010	$ 40,050	$ 52,062	77.4%	$ 726	$ 895	81.2%
2011	$ 39,068	$ 50,734	77.0%	$ 720	$ 876	82.2%
2012	$ 38,962	$ 50,929	76.5%	$ 712	$ 881	80.9%
2013	$ 39,792	$ 50,845	78.3%	$ 717	$ 874	82.1%
2014				$ 719	$ 871	82.5%

Chapter Six

Religious Diversity and the Public School Systems

CHAPTER OBJECTIVES

This chapter engages the place of religion in the US public school system. It addresses constitutional arguments relating to religion in schools, and attempts to set forth a timeline depicting the struggles for freedom of religious expression on school grounds dating back to the colonial days. The chapter explains the distinctions between the Establishment Clause and the Free Exercise Clause in the First Amendment to the US Constitution, and analyzes their implications for religious freedom in the United States. It discusses the challenges posed by rights to religious expression in schools, especially as it pertains to Muslim students in America's schools.

INTRODUCTION

A fundamental question that has plagued the American educational system in the last few decades has to do with the place of religion in the school systems, especially in the public school system. Some people from the Religious Right in America are always claiming a right to religious expression within the school grounds, while some from the Liberal Left are always arguing against it. Individuals from each faction often cross over in sympathy with one view or the other.

Probably the most reliable statement that can be made about the place of religion in the US public schools is that Americans are confused about the place of religion in the public school system. In order to engage this topic, we need to begin by addressing the question, "What place does religion have in the American public schools?"

Chapter Six

WHAT PLACE DOES RELIGION HAVE IN THE AMERICAN PUBLIC SCHOOL?

The United States of America is a constitutional democracy, in which the structures and powers of government are set and limited within the confines of a constitution. In a constitutional democracy, the power and authority of the majority is contained and limited by means of legal and institutional means in order to respect and protect the rights of individuals and minorities within the society.[1]

The implication this bears for America is that, despite the fact that America is a nation built on the Christian heritage and norms, the United States is not a religious state, and it cannot be technically classified as a Christian nation despite being a majority-Christian country. The First Amendment of the US Constitution declares as follows:

> *Congress shall make no law respecting an establishment of religion, or prohibiting the free exercise thereof; or abridging the freedom of speech, or of the press; or the right of the people peaceably to assemble, and to petition the government for a redress of grievances.*[2]

This article in the US Bill of Rights has become the bedrock of all kinds of controversies surrounding the practice of religion in American public schools today. Individuals and interest groups across the nation have interpreted these statements differently, each group strongly favoring its own interpretation more than its opponents'. Interest groups who feel that their rights to exercise their religious rights, as well as groups and individuals who see it as their duty to ensure a school climate free of all kinds of religious dominance, have appealed to courts of law from time to time to interpret this statement and determine whether certain exercise of religious rights and/or practices are protected under this law.

A fundamental argument that must be given serious consideration appeals to an understanding of the contextual meaning of the legislation when it was made more than two centuries ago, as well as its contemporary significance for the America of the twenty-first century. When the founding fathers made the declaration that "Congress shall make no law respecting an establishment of religion," what did they mean? What was "religion" as it was practiced among the eighteenth-century settlers on the American frontier? Chief Justice Waite, delivering the opinion of the Supreme Court of the United States in *Reynolds vs. the United States* in 1878, stated categorically that "the word 'religion' is not defined in the Constitution," and that its meaning must then be derived from "no where more appropriately, we think, than to the history of the times in the midst of which the provision was adopted."[3]

Study would show that religion at that time was more of a diverse expression of Christianity rather than a multiplicity of religions as we have them today. The spirit of this amendment derives from the desire of those founding fathers whose forebears had escaped Europe as a result of religious persecution, and had settled in the New World in search of a place to worship their Christian God with no governmental interruption. The spirit of this amendment, therefore, was a desire to protect the rights of the various factions of the Christian church of that age, rather than limiting it.

By implication, they provided for the rights of people who might venture to depart from the Christian experience of faith in search of other forms of religious expression, respecting that as a God-given right since the call to the Christian faith itself requires an individual decision and response to God rather than a collective societal (peoples) movement. The spirit of this amendment practically takes a stance against an official state religion, while focusing much more on the rights of individuals to religious expression anywhere in society.

It should be pointed out that the crises of how to regulate religious activities in the public school system was not very much an issue for the earlier generation of Americans. Education was not a state program, but private and religious organizations ran the schools. Schools were community based, and most communities enjoyed religious homogeneity, so religion was very much a part of the educational programs.

In the twentieth and twenty-first centuries, however, the American religious landscapes have not only shifted, but educational programs have also transitioned from being overwhelmingly private and religious to public and secular. Communities have also become more diverse both ethnically and religiously, making diversity an issue to contend with in the school systems. America is no longer religiously homogeneous (one may even contend that it never was, considering the various religious practices of the Native Americans and the African slaves who were brought into this land in those days).

One must also submit to the fact that even among the settlers, the concept of religious and cultural homogeneity was a practical impossibility. A 2014 Religious Landscape Study by Pew Research Center surveyed more than 35,000 Americans across the fifty states. The finding revealed the religious composition of the United States in Table 6.1.

This study shows that while retaining its Christian majority, the United States is a religiously diverse nation, more diverse than any other nation on the face of the earth. The religious nature of this nation continues to press the question about what place religion should have in a government-controlled public school system. To engage this question, let's examine some historic developments that have shaped the contemporary climate of separation of religion and state.

Table 6.1. US Religious Groups by Tradition, Family, and Denomination

Christian 70.6%
    Evangelical Protestant–25.4%
    Mainline Protestant–14.7%
    Historically Black Protestant–6.5%
    Catholic–20.8%
    Mormon–1.6%
    Orthodox Christian–0.5%
    Jehovah's Witness–0.8%
Other Christian–0.4%
Non-Christian Faiths–5.9%
    Jewish–1.9%
    Muslim–0.9%
    Buddhist–0.7%
    Hindu–0.7%
Other World Religions–0.3%
Other Faiths–1.5%
    Unaffiliated (religious "nones")–22.8%
    Atheist–3.1%
    Agnostic–4.0%
    Nothing in particular–15.8%
Don't know–0.6%

(Source: Pew Research Center, 2015)

Over the years, some courts have interpreted the First Amendment more rigorously, making a clear distinction between the first (Establishment Clause) and the second (Free Exercise Clause) parts that address religious rights, while others have been more tempered in their interpretation. A more general interpretation is that while the government cannot establish a religion or favor an established religion, the government cannot limit the rights of citizens to practice religion. In *Reynolds v. the United States*, one of the earliest judicial interpretations of the First Amendment is given with very strong historical backing.

In this case, Justice Waite and his colleagues stated that:

Before the adoption of the constitution, attempts were made in some of the colonies and states to legislate not only in respect to the establishment of religion, but in respect to its doctrines and precepts as well. The people were taxed, against their will, for the support of religion, and sometimes for the support of particular sects to whose tenets they could not subscribe. Punishments were prescribed for a failure to attend upon public worship, and sometimes for entertaining heretical opinions. . . . At the first session of the Congress the amendment now under consideration was proposed with others by Mr. Madison. It met the views of the advocates of religious freedom, and was adopted. Mr. Jefferson afterwards, in reply to an address to him by a committee of the Danbury Baptist

Association, took occasion to say: "Believing with you that religion is a matter which lies solely between man and his god; that he owes account to none other for his faith or his worship; that the legislative powers of the government reach actions only, and not opinion,—I contemplate with sovereign reverence that act of the whole American people which declared that their legislature should 'make no law respecting an establishment of religion or prohibiting the free exercise thereof,' thus building a wall of separation between church and state."[4]

The implications these statements bear on our understanding of the First Amendment is that it aimed at the preservation of individual's right to religious expression, as well as precludes the government from favoring one religious expression over another. This makes valid the judicial interpretation of the Establishment Clause and the Free Exercise Clause. They are separate but closely related entities.

It appears that the crises of interpreting the First Amendment has been primarily due to the tendency of some government officials to part ways with the manner in which certain courts have interpreted that law. Granted that the US Constitution empowers the judicial branch of the government to interpret the laws, there often arises a conflict in their interpretation and the manner in which some state and federal executives, whose function is the execution of the laws, seem to see it. This may be the reason why every administration in power wants to fill the courts with justices who share their own views on most issues.

The 1963 case of *Abington School District v. Schempp*, 374 U.S. 203[5] is a classic example of this dichotomy. The case centered on the fact that the commonwealth of Pennsylvania instituted a law (24Pa. Stat.15-1516) that was further amended in December 1959 to require the following: "At least ten verses from the Holy Bible Shall be read, without comment, at the opening of each public school on each day. Any child shall be excused from such Bible reading, or attending such Bible reading, upon the written request of his parent or guardian" (Pub. Law 1928, Supp. 1960).

Mr. Edward Kemp, his wife, and two children filed a suit against the state arguing that such a law violated their First Amendment rights, since they were practicing Unitarians. The trial courts ruled to their favor, and this case made its way to the US Supreme Court. The Supreme Court, in its interpretation of the First Amendment in the context of this case, stated that:

> ... *this court has rejected unequivocally the contention that the Establishment Clause forbids only governmental preferences of one religion over another. Almost 20 years ago in Everson, supra, at 15, the court said that "[n]either a state nor the Federal Government can set up a church. Neither can pass laws, which aid one religion, aid all religions, or prefer one religion over another."*[6]

This interpretation of the Constitution is as far-reaching as can be. Should this interpretation be accepted, George W. Bush's attempt to provide government funding to religious organizations involved in charity activities in the early 2000s would be deemed unconstitutional and illegal, since in a way it was aimed at aiding all religions who were involved in charity work. In this and other similar cases, the Supreme Court and lower trial courts have tried to hold on to a neutrality stance as much as governmental involvement in religion is concerned.

As part of the No Child Left Behind mandate, the US Department of Education, under President George W. Bush's mandate, issued guidelines for constitutionally protected prayer in schools. A full copy of the guidelines is obtainable from the US Department of Education's website. A section of the guideline addressed the government's interpretation of the Establishment Clause, as well as the Free Exercise Clause:

> *Accordingly, the First Amendment forbids religious activity that is sponsored by the government but protects religious activity that is initiated by private individuals, and the line between government-sponsored and privately initiated religious expression is vital to a proper understanding of the First Amendment's scope. As the Court has explained in several cases, "there is a crucial difference between **government** speech endorsing religion, which the Establishment Clause forbids, and **private** speech endorsing religion, which the Free Speech and Free Exercise Clauses protect."*[7]

Whereas some courts see the role of the government as that of complete neutrality, other courts and government officials see their role as that of protection of religious rights. The government position also argues that the First Amendment does not forbid religious activities initiated by private citizens whether in public or private, thus making the case that whereas the government may not sponsor religion, religion has a place in the American public life if the citizens choose to exercise such rights. Under President Bill Clinton,[8] a guideline was issued to the public schools, which stated that:

> *The Establishment Clause of the First Amendment does not prohibit religious speech by students. Students, therefore, have the same right to engage in individual or group prayer and religious discussion during the school day as they do to engage in other comparable activity.*[9]

Compared to George W. Bush's stand, it is significant that two ideologically opposed administrations seem to agree on this one issue. This means that, depending on who is in the Oval Office, the executive branch of the government is inclined to reject any court interpretation of the First Amendment that defines neutrality as staying away from the realm of religion. In fact, the subsequent two administrations have retained the same guidelines from the Bush administration. In this light, therefore, religion will continue to be an integral part of American government and the American public school system.

WHERE IN THE PUBLIC SCHOOL CURRICULUM DOES RELIGION BELONG?

One of the hot-button topics when it comes to religion in schools in the United States is the teaching of evolution in schools. There is a wide chasm between those with a religious worldview that subscribe to a literal interpretation of the book of Genesis in the Bible, and those who hold on to a strictly scientific and evolutionary explanation of the origin of life.

A study by LifeWay Research Center shows a very strong literal biblical view of the origin of life among Protestant pastors (see Figure 6.1). This reflects what they teach and what they propagate among their parishioners. Given the very strong Protestant/Evangelical presence in the United States, it is understandable why the topic of evolution has continued to generate intense controversies within the educational settings.

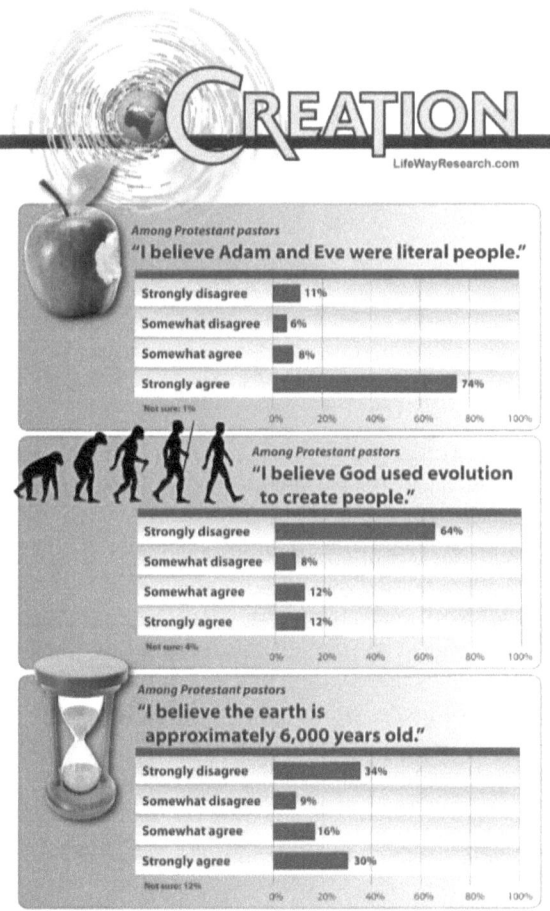

Figure 6.1. Lifeway Survey on Evolution

A 2013 Pew Research Center study shows the views of the general population of US citizens on this matter of evolution and creationism (see Figure 6.2). The study asked US adults whether they believed that humans and other living things in their present forms existed since the beginning of time, or whether they have evolved over time. The result showed an overall 60 percent belief in evolution, with 33 percent believing that human and other lives have existed in their present forms from the beginning of time. White and black evangelicals, however, showed a higher degree of belief in creationism than the rest of the religious groups sampled.

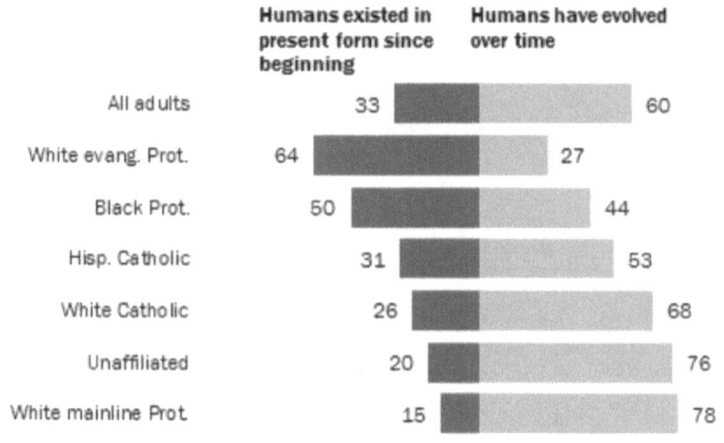

Figure 6.2. Religious Views about Human Origin

From the scientific front, however, 98 percent of scientists affiliated with the American Association for the Advancement of Science held that human and other lives evolved over time (see Figure 6.3).

So, the controversy over religion in schools continues on the area of curriculum and instruction as it relates to evolution and creationism, yet that's just one of the many fronts where the battle over religion in schools is being waged.

For most educators and politicians, as well as parents and students, the fact that religion has a place in the public school system raises another question, namely, where specifically in the school system should it belong? Two documents on Guidelines on constitutionally protected prayer in schools from both

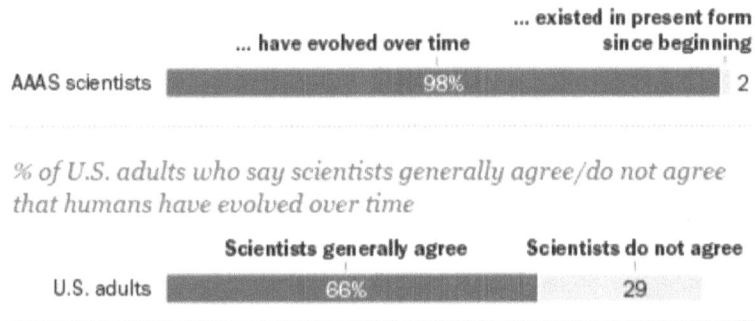

Figure 6.3. Scientific Views on Human Origin

Clinton and Bush administrations provided detailed guidelines on the nature of religious programs that students could carry out while in school.

Their definition of government neutrality is seen in the need for government officials while acting in their official capacity to refrain from leading, initiating, or participating in any religious activity. They cannot, however, prevent students from engaging in religious activity during school hours. Students are empowered to use school facilities to the degree that other nonreligious clubs in the schools use these facilities to hold their prayer services, worship exercises, or Bible studies. Students are free to distribute religious flyers in the schools, to the extent that other nonreligious clubs have rights to do.

They are entitled to use school public address systems to advertise their events, to the extent that other nonreligious clubs are allowed to do. Students can be excused from class to engage in a religious activity over a brief period of time, like Muslim students who need to pray during Ramadan.

Some significant issues are addressed in one of these documents that are not addressed in the other. The Bush document addressed the need to allow for moments of silence if the school should choose to implement one. It discouraged teachers and school administrators from encouraging or discouraging prayers during this time.

The two documents each addressed the right of the students to express a religious belief in homework, artwork, and other written or oral assignments. The work was to be judged on the basis of its academic content, not its religious merit. Students should be allowed to distribute religious literature to their fellow students to the degree that they could distribute other materials.

The Bush document emphasized the neutral role of the teachers and administrators in leading or participating in a religious activity with students. It also provided for teachers and administrators to be able to "take part in religious activities where the overall context makes clear that they are not participating in their official capacities." Before school or during lunch, for example, teachers may meet with other teachers for prayer or Bible study to the same extent that they may engage in other conversations or nonreligious activities. It suggests that teachers may participate in their personal capacities in privately sponsored baccalaureate ceremonies.[10]

The Clinton document addressed, in addition, the issue of teaching about religion in the school curriculum. It stipulated that public schools may not provide religious instruction, but may teach about religion, "including the Bible or other scriptures: the history of religion, comparative religion, the Bible (or other scripture)—as literature and the role of religion in the history of the United States and other countries."[11]

Evolution is one topic that is conspicuously absent in both documents, yet it remains one of the most controversial topics when Americans discuss the place of religion in the public school curriculum.

CONSTITUTIONAL PROVISIONS FOR STUDENTS' AND TEACHERS' RIGHTS TO RELIGIOUS EXPRESSION

Morning Prayers

School administrators and teachers cannot mandate a morning prayer. Such would be an attempt to advance religion, and it significantly departs from the neutral stance of government. A moment of silence may, however, be observed, and students may choose to pray during this time or not to pray.

Prayers at Athletic Events

The government position states that students reserve the right to initiate such prayers, but they cannot be mandated to do so by the school authority. A school would also be violating the neutrality stance if it chooses the event leader based on the likelihood to pray or not to pray.

Prayers at Graduation Ceremonies

Prayers are acceptable if they are initiated by students and not faculty. There is an ambiguity as to what the teachers should do, in an official school activity like games or graduation, when a student initiates a prayer and other people join in. The most popular position is that teachers should not participate. They are never to join the students in religious activities during their official work hours. After official hours, they can join.

THE PLACE OF ISLAM IN THE AMERICAN EDUCATIONAL SETTING

Since the attack on the World Trade Center on September 11, 2001, the place of Islam as a religion in the United States has taken a different form, characterized by controversy and tension in all public spaces. The place of Islam in US schools has become increasingly a topic of tension.

The history of Islam in the United States traces back to the early days of the transatlantic slave trade. Some African slaves who were brought to the New World from the West African coast were of Muslim heritage. The number of Muslims in the United States has increased exponentially through the influx of refugees from war-torn countries like Somalia, Iraq, Syria, and other parts of the world. Many Muslims have also immigrated to the United States through the normal channels of education, trade, and other commercial activities.

As of the year 2017, the Pew Research Center estimated that the number of Muslims in the United States was about 3.45 million, an increase of 1.1 million from 2007.[12] Figure 6.4 shows the trend.

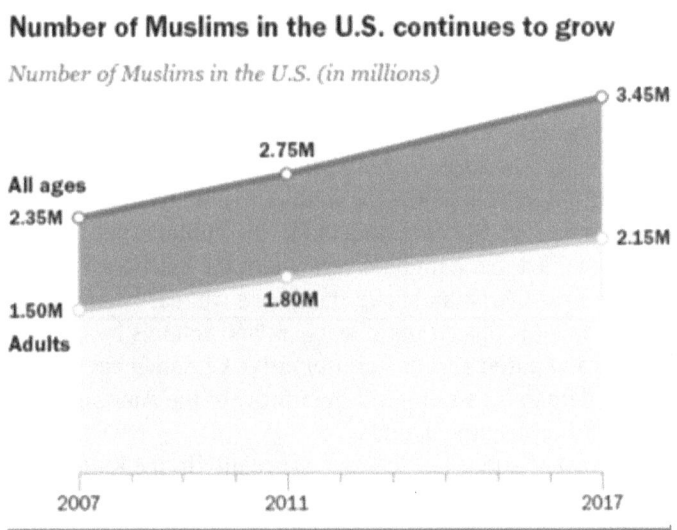

Figure 6.4. Number of Muslims in the United States

Islam in the United States today has been described as highly misunderstood, given that many Americans hold views that have been described by some Muslims as inaccurate and negative perceptions of Islam.[13] The challenges facing Islam in the US educational setting have been described as a variety of negative responses that span from outright racism to rejection or the minimization of Muslim perspectives and contributions to education and society.

A 2015 study by Van der Noll and Saroglou speculated that what has been interpreted as anti-Islamic tendencies in the West may have been caused by a more general resentment of religion, which has become widespread in the Western societies as people are beginning to advocate for stricter separation between religion and state.

Some of the by-products of these negative experiences in the public school setting have led to various responses and reactions from the Muslim communities, among which is the exponential growth of private Islamic schools in the United States and Canada. A tension that has arisen from these reactions to the public school experiences includes increasing anti-Westernizing tendencies, the religious and nativist radicalization of Muslim youth, and growing competing views of education, life, and society.[14]

US public schools, however, have struggled continuously to make proper accommodations for Muslim students. It is important to note that while the Christian religion constitutes the largest proportion of religious affiliations in the United States, the demands of the Christian community for religious accommodation in schools are minimal and clear-cut. Those Christians who demand accommodation do so with respect to the right to pray, read the holy Scriptures, and freely express their religious views. Even among the Christian population, there is a wide divide as some Christians don't want religion in the school setting.

The accommodation of the needs of Muslim students, however, may not be as simple and clear-cut as those of their Christian peers. In a document titled *An Educator's Guide to Islamic Religious Practices* (2005), the Council on American-Islamic Relations listed the items in Table 6.2 as accommodations that need to be made for Muslim students in the public school setting.

Considering the fact that a high percentage of the teachers in the US public schools come from a Christian background, one can easily see a negative response to the mandates placed upon teachers and schools by these demands. Some educators and parents from a conservative Christian background would easily see these demands as a cultural overthrow of the American educational system in favor of an Islamic agenda.

The fact, however, is that US schools, especially in the K–12 setting, have not done a very good job of educating students on the positive benefits of

Table 6.2.

Pork and Pork By-Products in Lunches	Mark Items with a Red Dot or a Picture of a Pig.
Muslim holidays	Schedule exams and other major events around holidays. Do not mark students absent.
Ramadan fast	Allow students to study in the library or elsewhere during lunch.
Physical education	Discuss clothing requirements with Muslim parents. Reschedule classes for students preferring same-gender exercise environment.
Gender relations	Do not extend hand first for handshake with opposite sex. Avoid touching when comforting students and parents of opposite sex.
Family life/sex education program	Allow parents reasonable time to review any material dealing with "sex education." Allow children to opt-out from all or part of the family life program.
Prayer	Allow Muslim students to pray in unused rooms. Practice fairness in classroom and text presentations. Check textbooks for religious bias. Invite Muslim speakers to social studies and world religion classes.

diversity, be it religious or cultural. When schools are able to spend time educating their students and families on the positive contributions of Muslims in the fields of science, medicine, education, and other fields, the need to accommodate their religious needs in the public school setting will no longer be seen as a threat.[15]

NOTABLE US COURT CASES ON RELIGION IN SCHOOLS

In this section, legal briefs on a few important court cases involving religious freedom in the US schools will be highlighted. Beginning with a 1952 court ruling, and continuing all the way to April 2018, these cases will address the broad topics covered in this chapter, ranging from prayer in schools to curriculum, and to religious diversity issues.

Case #1: Zorach v. Clauson (1952)

Citation:

Zorach v. Clauson (1952), No. 431, Argued: January 31 and February 1, 1952, Decided: April 28, 1952[16]

Facts about the Case:

Some taxpayers in the state of New York, whose children attended the New York Public Schools, filed a lawsuit challenging the school system's involvement in the religious pullout program. They contended that the weight and influence of the school system was being used to support the program of religious instruction when public school teachers were used to facilitate it by releasing students from class and keeping tab on those students who were released, and when classroom activities were halted due to the release of some students for religious instruction. They argued that the religious programs would be futile and ineffective if the school's cooperation was withdrawn. In effect, their argument claimed that the government through the New York public school system was facilitating the establishment of religion.

The Issue in Question:

The primary issue in question as determined by the court in this case was whether New York City Public Schools had, through their pullout religious instruction program, prohibited the free exercise of religion or made a law respecting the establishment of religion, within the meaning of these two clauses in the First Amendment.

Previous History:

A good historic case would be *McCollum v. Board of Education*, 333 US 203 (1948), in Champaign County, Illinois, a case that was decided on March 8, 1948. The school system had granted permission to religious groups, including Catholics, Protestants, and Jews, to come to the school once a week and provide religious instruction to students whose parents had granted permission for them to be excused from their regular secular classes to attend religious instruction. A parent of a child in the district and resident taxpayer of the school district sued for a writ of mandamus, demanding the board of education terminate the religious instruction program. A writ of mandamus was denied to the plaintiff, as the court argued that "to hold that a state cannot, consistently with the First and Fourteenth Amendments, utilize its public school system to aid any or all religious faiths or sects in the dissemination of their doctrines and ideals does not, as counsel urge, manifest a governmental hostility to religion or religious teachings. A manifestation of such hostility would be at war with our national tradition as embodied in the First Amendment's guaranty of the free."[17] The appellants in *Zorach v. Clauson* argued that the New York City situation was not unlike the case in *McCollum v. Board of Education*.

Holding:

The US Supreme Court held that the practice in the state of New York did not violate the First Amendment.

Reasoning:

The Court reasoned that the practice in the New York Public Schools did not prohibit the free exercise of religion, neither did it make a law respecting the establishment of religion within the meanings of the First Amendment. Also, they reasoned that there was no evidence to support the claim that the system used coercion to get public school students to participate in religious instruction.

Significance:

The significance of this case lies in the fact that the way the courts have interpreted the First Amendment in this case warrants a careful interpretation of the Jeffersonian comment on a "Wall of Separation" between church and state. That wall must never be viewed as a concrete wall, as the First Amendment does not suggest an absolute lack of intersection between the state and religion, but rather focuses on the need for the state to desist from acting through legislation or otherwise to foster or hinder religion. It suggests a neutrality that does not necessarily imply no intersection. Given that both the state and religion stand to serve the citizens, the two are bound to cross paths one way or the other.

Case # 2: Engel v. Vitale *(1962)*

Citation:

Engel v. Vitale (1962). No. 468. Argued: April 3, 1962, Decided: June 25, 1962

Facts about the Case:

The board of regents of the state of New York had authorized a short prayer to be recited at the start of each school day. This prayer was not mandatory, but voluntary. The prayer read as follows: "Almighty God, we acknowledge our dependence upon Thee, and beg Thy blessings upon us, our teachers, and our country."[18] Following the adopting of this prayer by the regents of the state, parents of ten students in the New York school system filed a lawsuit in a New York state court arguing that adoption of this official prayer for use in the public schools was contrary to their beliefs, religions, or religious practices, as well as those of their children. They challenged the law authorizing the use of prayer in public schools as well as the school district's regulation ordering the recitation of this particular prayer on the grounds that these actions were of official governmental agencies, which they claimed violated the First Amendment of the United States Constitution. The lower courts ruled to uphold the rights of the school district to allow the prayer as long as the schools did not compel students to join in the prayer against their will or their parents' consent. The New York Appeals Court upheld the lower court's ruling.

The Issue in Question:

The issue in question in this case was whether the reading of a nondenominational prayer at the start of the school day violated the First Amendment's Establishment of Religion clause.[19]

Previous History:

The historical facts considered by the judges in this case went as far back as the early days of the American colonies, when men who fled religious persecution in England began to establish religion in the American colonies as soon as they had gained some political prowess. It considered the oppositions mounted by minority religious bodies in the colonies, such as the Presbyterians, the Baptists, the Lutherans, and the Quakers, who combined forces and lobbied James Madison and Thomas Jefferson between 1785 and 1786 to help enact the famous "Virginia Bill for Religious Liberty" placing all religious groups on an equal footing, and opposing government establishment of religion.[20]

Holding:

The US Supreme Court held that this New York law violated the First Amendment's Establishment Clause. They reversed the ruling by the state appeals court, and remanded it for further proceedings not inconsistent with their opinion.

Reasoning:

The court's reasoning was that neither the nondenominational character of the prayer, nor its voluntary character, protected it from being unconstitutional. They reasoned that in providing the prayer, the state had officially approved religion.

Significance:

This case has become the basis upon which many previously allowed religious practices in US schools have been eliminated. The Establishment Clause was given a new life and strength by this ruling, and the courts have interpreted it following this ruling in ways that have been unfavorable to religious rights and practices in schools. *Engel v. Vitale* has remained the most resented court ruling among Americans who value religious rights. Many new court rulings have also anchored decisions on this ruling, the most significant of which was *Lemon v. Kurtzman* in 1971, in which the Supreme Court adopted a three-prong "test" for determining whether laws violated the Establishment Clause. They ruled that for a law to be constitutional, it must a) have a secular legislative purpose, b) neither advance nor inhibit religion, and c) not foster an excessive government entanglement with religion.[21]

Case #3: **Edwards v. Aguillard *(1987)***

Citation:

Edwards v. Aguillard (1987), No. 85-1513. Argued: December 10, 1986, Decided: June 19, 1987

Facts about the Case:

This case pertains to a Louisiana law (Louisiana's "Creationism Act"),[22] that prohibited the teaching of the theory of evolution in the public schools unless the instruction was also accompanied by the teaching of creation science. Creation science is a Bible-based belief that advances an abrupt appearance of life on earth. The law required that if teachers must teach one of the two theories, they must also teach the other one.[23] A group of teachers, parents, and religious leaders in Louisiana filed a suit in a federal district court, seeking injunctions and declaratory relief.

The Issue in Question:

The issue before the court was to determine whether this law violated the Establishment Clause of the First Amendment to the US Constitution as applied to the states through the Fourteenth Amendment.

Previous History:

In deciding this case, the appeals court called to bear the fact that the court has often been required to invalidate statutes that advance religion in public elementary and secondary schools contrary to the freedoms outlined in the First Amendment. Such cases as *Grand Rapids School District v. Ball*, supra, which pertained to school district's use of religious school teachers in public schools, and *Wallace v. Jaffree*, supra in Alabama, which authorized a moment of silence for school prayer, were used as historical precedents in deciding this case.

Holding

The district court held that this Louisiana law violated the US Constitution. The appeals court upheld the ruling from the lower court.

Reasoning

The courts' reasoning included the fact that the law was invalid because it violated the Establishment Clause of the First Amendment. The court judged that the law lacked a clear secular purpose, and that it did not protect academic freedom, which the appellant claimed was the law's intent. The law was seen as endorsing religion, since it effectively sought to advance a religious view.

Significance:

The ruling in this case has been read as a Supreme Court defeat of the anti-evolution forces.[24] Arguably, this case has served to stem the tide of pressures from the Religious Right to infuse creationism into the public school science curriculum.

Chapter Seven

The Challenge of Poverty in Twenty-First-Century America

CHAPTER OBJECTIVES

This chapter engages poverty as an important issue in multicultural education. Every child comes to the K–12 classroom with a measure of social and economic capital. Some are better equipped than others with the social and economic resources they need to succeed in school. In this chapter, poverty is discussed as a global issue, but more attention is given to poverty in the United States and the various ways government policies and practices have helped to create poverty or mitigate it.

POVERTY: A GLOBAL PROBLEM

Poverty can be simply defined as the lack of basic necessities of life to meet the needs of food, shelter, clothing, warmth, and a sense of safety. This definition covers mostly physical needs without necessarily attempting to align with Maslow's hierarchy of needs. What constitutes poverty in many societies is basic and simple, yet a large percentage of human populations lack these basic and simple items.

The World Bank estimates that 1.44 billion of the world's population live in extreme poverty. They defined extreme poverty within the confines of financial health, suggesting that one is living in extreme poverty if the individual lives on an average of US$1.25 a day. The concept of extreme poverty, however, implies more than a lack of money or other material resources. When an individual lacks the opportunity to make meaningful choices to sustainably improve his or her life, that person is living in extreme poverty.[1]

In the United States, the Federal Government Poverty Guideline serves to determine eligibility for Medicaid and for the Children's Health Insurance Program (CHIP). Within these guidelines, poverty is defined by income level. So poverty is defined as the lack of sufficient money to meet one's basic needs.[2] The Oxford Poverty and Human Development Initiative (OPHI) asserts that this kind of definition of poverty is one-dimensional, and does not capture the multiple factors that constitute poverty. According to OPHI, people in poverty do not define their conditions with single factors or in one dimension; instead they define them with multidimensional factors. Some of the factors used by people in poverty to define their condition include nutrition, health, lack of adequate sanitation, social exclusion, lack of clean water, low education, violence, bad housing conditions, shame, and disempowerment, among many other factors.[3] The primary elements of multidimensional poverty is shown in Figure 7.1.

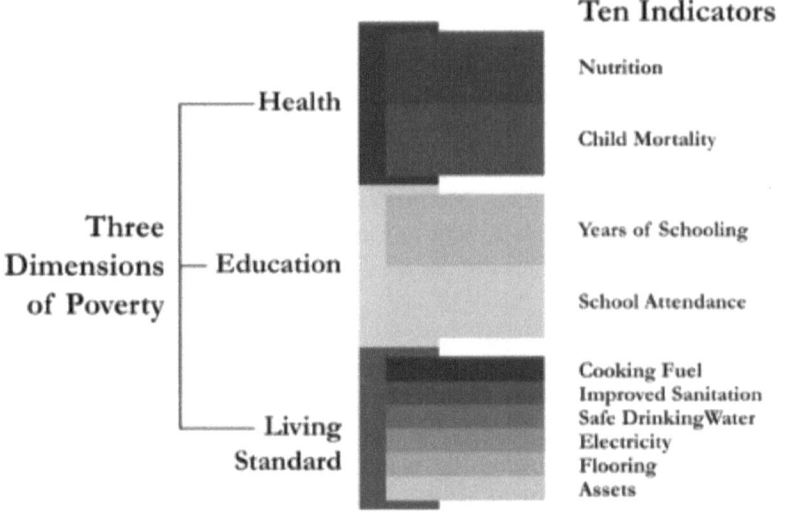

Figure 7.1. Elements of Multidimensional Poverty

A 2017 Global Multidimensional Poverty Index (MPI) showed that 1.46 billion people on earth were "multidimensionally" poor. The same study showed some key findings on Global MPI:

- Forty-eight percent of the poor people live in South Asia, and 36 percent of them live in sub-Saharan Africa.
- Most MPI poor people (72 percent of them) live in what are considered middle-income countries.

- Half of the multidimensionally poor people are children ages 0–17 (48 percent of multidimensionally poor people).
- Nearly half of all MPI poor people are destitute (about 706 million), so they experience extreme deprivations such as severe malnutrition in at least one-third of the dimensions.
- In Uganda, for example, 22 percent of people live in a household where at least one person has a severe disability. Poverty in such households is higher, with 77 percent of these people poor, compared to 69 percent in other households.[4]

Using the OPHI MPI as a guide, one can see that the United Nations' definition of poverty expands beyond an insufficient amount of money for meeting one's basic needs to include other factors that are caused by or accompany poverty, such as food insecurity, lack of proper health and nutrition, poor maternal health for pregnant women, mortality and causes of death, exposure to violence, displacement, refugee status, and migration. The global statistics on extreme poverty levels seem to be even higher this year, with NURU International projecting 1.6 billion people living in extreme poverty, with 85 percent of those living in rural communities.

A recent report by the United Nations Human Rights Council showed that 40 million citizens and residents of the United States live in poverty. More than half of these people were identified as living in "extreme" or "absolute" poverty.[5] This damning report exposed the fact that the United States has the highest child mortality rate of all the twenty richest countries. The United States, with a 21 percent child poverty rate, is among the countries with the highest child poverty rates in the developed world.[6]

When compared with other developed nations, relative child poverty rates range from 5 percent in Norway to over 20 percent in the United States, with the United States being among the nations with the highest poverty rates. Study showed that the child poverty rate in the United States stands at twice that of the United Kingdom, Sweden, and France.[7] A common factor in the US poverty rate is the fact of underemployment, in which individuals may be working at two to three jobs, yet unable to make ends meet due to underemployment and lack of adequate income and benefits to alleviate the effects of poverty.

A recent study revealed that 40 percent of the adult population in the United States who were interviewed stated that they would not be able to cover an unexpected expense of $400. A January 14, 2018, *New York Times* article estimated that half of college students in the United States struggle with food insecurity. The report indicts the Trump administration for stigmatizing the poor in the United States as lazy, when the percentage of those receiving public help in the United States and not working is only 7 percent.[8]

The US government uses a one-dimensional indicator for determining poverty level in the United States, and that indicator is financial income. The US 2017 Poverty Index is shown in Table 7.1.

Table 7.1. US 2017 Poverty Index

Household Size	100%	133%	150%	200%	250%	300%	400%
1	$12,060	$16,040	$18,090	$24,120	$30,150	$36,180	$48,240
2	16,240	21,599	24,360	32,480	40,600	48,720	64,960
3	20,420	27,159	30,630	40,840	51,050	61,260	81,680
4	24,600	32,718	36,900	49,200	61,500	73,800	98,400
5	28,780	38,277	43,170	57,560	71,950	86,340	115,120
6	32,960	43,837	49,440	65,920	82,400	98,880	131,840
7	37,140	49,396	55,710	74,280	92,850	111,420	148,560
8	41,320	54,956	61,980	82,640	103,300	123,960	165,280

The Federal Poverty Guidelines are issued annually by the Department of Health and Human Services. A new guideline is issued in January of each year for the year in which it is issued. These guidelines are used to determine people's eligibility for certain federal government programs such as Medicaid and the Children's Health Insurance Program.[9]

Child Poverty in the United States

The implications of poverty for multicultural education lies in the fact that children often bear the larger brunt of poverty across the globe. A 2017 estimate by UNICEF had 19.5 percent of the world's children living in extreme poverty, compared to only 9.2 percent of adults in extreme poverty. The report showed that more children than adults across most OECD countries live in extreme poverty. In sub-Saharan Africa, for example, 66.2 percent of the extremely poor are children, and in South Asia, the number is 49.5 percent.[10] Nearly 58 percent of children who live in areas of the world that are threatened by such political instability as inadequate national economic management, lack of policies to combat inequity, and a weak civil society, are affected by extreme poverty.[11]

According to the National Center for Children in Poverty (NCPP), 21 percent of all US children (about 15 million) live in families whose income is below the Federal Poverty Threshold. The Federal Poverty Threshold is defined as a specified dollar amount that is considered the minimum level of financial resources required to meet the basic needs of a family unit.[12] A national study on income shows that 41 percent of all American children live in homes considered to be low income, with only 59 percent living in

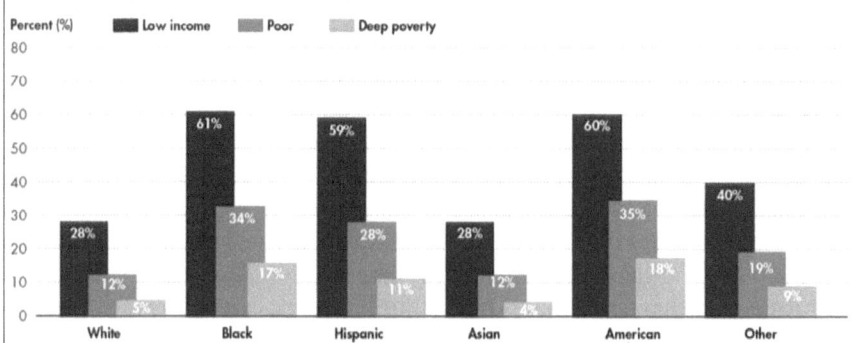

Figure 7.2. Percentage of Low Income and Poor Families by Race and Ethnicity

homes considered above the low income level.[13] Of the 41 percent with a low income, 19 percent are poor, while 22 percent are near poor.

According to NCPP, poverty can negatively impact a child's ability to learn. Poverty contributes to social, emotional, and behavioral problems that children may face at home and at school. It can also lead to poor physical and mental health. All of these factors contribute to affect academic performance and drive up the achievement gap between the child in poverty and his/her peers who are not in poverty. African Americans, Native Americans, and Hispanics seem to constitute the largest proportion of poor children in the United States (see Figure 7.2).

Given the known effects of poverty on learning and academic performance, this could also offer some explanation for the achievement gaps between these groups and their white counterparts. A large proportion of low-income children and youth, and their families, are affected by mental health issues and challenges, leading to impairment in the ability of these children and youth to succeed in school. Poverty, therefore, places them at risk of failure, and the risk of falling into the cracks of involvement in the child welfare and juvenile justice systems.[14]

A HISTORY OF POVERTY IN THE UNITED STATES

One can easily make a strong case that poverty in the United States has been constructed by the combined forces of economic realities and individual and institutional racism. The early days of the life in the New World was a period of upward mobility, when immigrants would come in from Europe with only a piece of cloth on their backs; they would work hard, earn a living, and often pull themselves up from poverty to wealth. Americans have this common story about their ancestors: "My father came from . . . (mostly Western European countries), worked hard, and pulled himself up by his bootstraps."

This narrative speaks to the abundance of opportunities for those new Americans who were willing to work hard and pull themselves up out of poverty. What this narrative often misses is the fact that there were other immigrants who did not even have boots whose straps they could use to pull themselves up. These euphoric immigrant narratives were happening when the original dwellers of this land were being dispossessed of land, life, liberty, and the pursuit of happiness. Since their displacement, the larger bulk of Native Americans have lived lives of destitution and poverty.

The African slaves who were brought here also were not allowed access to this common immigrant bootstrap narrative. Slavery robbed them of the right to life, liberty, and the pursuit of anything. They lived and died at the whim of their slave masters. They toiled from day to night to earn a living for their slave masters just as a mule would do. They had no right to any portion of the proceeds of their labors, but they ate or drank only at the mercy of their slave masters. Even after the Emancipation Proclamation, they had no land or property to build a life upon, so those who wanted to work had neither land nor crops of their own, and they were easily re-enslaved through the sharecropping injustices that followed the end of slavery.

With the end of the Civil War, many Southern states passed Jim Crow laws, which strictly restricted the rights of blacks to access job opportunities, public services, and other resources that could propel an upward economic mobility. Many blacks who are living today have parents, grandparents, and great-grandparents who lived under Jim Crow laws. Even those blacks who were able to work hard and earn resources to pull themselves out of poverty were restricted on where they could live, as federal government policies such as redlining prevented them from investing in good real estate markets to build wealth.

Even after World War II, the New Deal that created American suburbia refused opportunities to blacks and other minorities for good education, housing, and employment, even as it made lofty promises to white citizens and then delivered on these promises. The New Deal created the American middle class and suburbia, but that middle class did not include blacks, Hispanics, or Native Americans. So, effectively, government exclusionary practices created generational poverty that has continue to haunt many black, Hispanic, and Native American families until today.

The faces of poverty in twenty-first-century America, however, is not only black and brown. J. D. Vance in his *Hillbilly Elegy* (2016) documents a telling narrative of poverty that has become almost normative of the Appalachian region. Vance describes a white population that is marrying less and divorcing more, a people whose economic opportunities have dwindled due to a number of factors, among which is the decline of America's manufacturing industries.

He described this group of whites as socially isolated; even when they lose their jobs they often choose to not relocate to find new jobs, so many have dropped out of the labor market. This region has also suffered heavily under the weight of the illicit drug abuse and prescription drug addiction that has ravaged the entire nation. The statistics on national overdose death from opioids in 2017 is above 49,000 (see Figure 7.3).

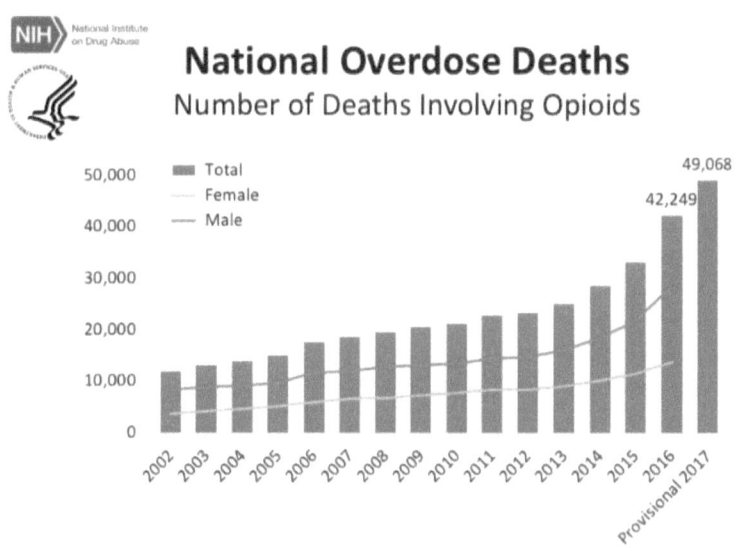

Figure 7.3. Deaths from Opioid Overdose

According to Vance, many Americans today spend their way into the poorhouse. They buy giant TVs and iPads, and their children wear nice clothes purchased on high-interest credit cards and payday loans. They purchase homes they don't need, and they refinance them to collect more spending money, only to declare bankruptcy soon after that. He calls them a population to whom thrift has become inimical to their being.

This point is made to state that in addition to the historic injustices that created generational poverty, along with those who have become poor due to economic policies that have adversely affected the working class, some are poor in American today as a result of self-inflicted injuries that come from addiction to comfort and enjoyments that they cannot afford. So effectively, the faces of poverty in twenty-first-century America are white, black, and brown. The ethnicity of poverty is white, African American, Asian, Hispanic,

Native American, and others. So the conversation on poverty in the United States needs to be varied and all-encompassing.

THE UNITED NATIONS ON POVERTY

In September 2000, 191 UN member states agreed that by the year 2015 they would achieve eight Millennium Development Goals. The goals were as follows:

1. to eradicate extreme poverty and hunger;
2. to achieve universal primary education;
3. to promote gender equality and empower women;
4. to reduce child mortality;
5. to improve maternal health;
6. to combat HIV/AIDS, malaria, and other diseases;
7. to ensure environmental sustainability; and
8. to develop a global partnership for development.[15]

It is noteworthy that the eradication of extreme poverty is at the top of this list. The United Nations defined extreme poverty as "a condition characterized by severe deprivation of basic human needs, including food, safe drinking water, sanitation facilities, health, shelter, education and information. It depends not only on income but also on access to services."[16] This definition came from the declaration of the World Summit for Social Development that was held in Copenhagen, Denmark, from September 6 to 12, 1995. At this summit, the attending nations stated the following:

> We heads of State and Government are committed to a political, economic, ethical and spiritual vision for social development that is based on human dignity, human rights, equality, respect, peace, democracy, mutual responsibility and cooperation, and full respect for the various religious and ethical values and cultural backgrounds of people. Accordingly, we will give the highest priority in national, regional and international policies and actions to the promotion of social progress, justice and the betterment of the human condition, based on full participation by all.[17]

In light of this commitment of the world's nations, let's briefly examine policies and actions that the United States government has taken over the years to address poverty and improve human conditions.

SOCIAL PROGRAMS TARGETING POVERTY IN THE UNITED STATES

A book titled *Down and Out in the Great Depression: Letters from the Forgotten Man*, edited by Robert S. McElvaine (1983), provides a peek into the lives of the poor during the Great Depression, and the nature of government responses and actions toward poverty alleviation. The book highlights the fact that an enduring historical view of poverty in the United States has been the tendency to see poverty as self-inflicted wounds that come from indolence, improvidence, and intemperance.

While recognizing that some among the poor are unfortunate, cannot care for themselves (the crippled, the blind, the elderly, the widowed, and the orphaned), and therefore should be helped, there has been a tendency to make the provision of charity rare and difficult to obtain, so as to discourage dependency. These attitudes have persisted over the years, and have affected government policies on poverty alleviation and social welfare. Against this backdrop, let's examine some historical poverty alleviation programs in the United States.

Social Welfare Programs

One study states that in 2009, publicly funded social welfare policy spending in the United States took 19.2 percent of the nation's GDP. This, however, does not suggest a liberal welfare system in the United States. A large chunk of this expense come from Social Security (a federal retirement pension program), social insurance programs (such as unemployment insurance), and social welfare programs that target the poor. The most basic welfare program aimed at the poor was the Aid to Families with Dependent Children (AFDC) program, which provided financial assistance to low-income single-parent families. This program was established in 1935 as part of the Social Security Act. Over the years, it suffered declining popularity as an increasing number of African American families gained eligibility for it.[18]

In 1996, the AFDC was abolished and replaced by what is now called Temporary Assistance for Needy Families (TANF) program. This new program imposed strict time limits on most recipients, making access rather difficult. President Bill Clinton bragged as he ended the AFDC in 1996, saying that he had ended the welfare program "as we know it."[19] According to Beland and Waddan (2017), a unique feature of the US welfare system is the absence of a universal public social program where entitlements to benefits and services are guaranteed on the basis of citizenship or residency.

In Canada and many European countries, citizenship and residency guarantees entitlement to social welfare programs, but many Americans, especially the wealthy, hate the idea of entitlement. Family benefits aimed at poverty alleviation require much more to access in the United States than just residency or citizenship. Belland and Waddan attribute the strict requirements for access to family programs to racism in the South, which created strong pressures in Congress for the preservation of state control over social-assistance family benefits as powerful tools of social and economic control that white elites could wield over blacks and other minorities.

The unpopularity of family programs aimed at poverty alleviation has increased since Ronald Reagan painted the image of the African American recipient as a "welfare queen." Contrary to public perception, however, only a very small percentage of federal welfare spending goes directly to needy families. In 2010, $689b of federal welfare spending went to Social Security, $519b went to Medicare, and $259b went to Medicaid, programs whose largest proportion of beneficiaries are white. Only $7b went directly to temporary assistance to needy families; $65b went to nutritional assistance (food stamps), and $10b went to school lunches.

It is significant that the combined spending on family assistance, food stamps, and school lunches, of $82b, is less than half of the money spent on unemployment compensation (see Table 7.2). The goal of needy-family support programs is to stabilize families, reduce unexpected crises, prevent children from suffering, and improve family functioning,[20] yet these values are forgotten when social welfare programs are politicized. According to Barany (2016), a behavioral paradigm that is tinged with racial and male patriarchal sentiments has combined to threaten the needy-family welfare program in the United States.

Public Housing Programs

The idea of public housing is something that has developed with the growth of American cities. History is unclear as to the real genesis of the idea of public housing to address urban poverty, but in 1867 the city of New York enacted the first tenement laws in the nation, banning the construction of rooms without ventilators and the construction of apartments without fire escapes in the city. This was probably the earliest attempt to improve the housing conditions of the poor within the city. Another important landmark was the construction of the first public housing project in the nation by the mayor of the city of Milwaukee in 1923, Mayor Daniel Hoan.[21]

In 1934, the National Housing Act was passed, establishing the Federal Housing Administration, and in 1937 the Congress passed the US Housing

Table 7.2. Federal Spending in 2010

Appendix Table: Spending in Fiscal Year 2010 for Programs Included in This Analysis (in billions of dollars)	Federal	State	Total
Mandatory spending (core analysis)			
Social Security [a]	689		689
Unemployment compensation [b]	156		156
Supplemental Security Income	44		44
Temporary Assistance for Needy Families (basic assistance only) [c]	7	4	11
Supplemental Nutrition Assistance Program [d]	65		65
School Lunches [e]	10		10
Earned Income Tax Credit (refundable share) [f]	55		55
Child Tax Credit (refundable share)	23		23
Medicare [g]	519		519
Medicaid [h]	259	123	382
Children's Health Insurance Program [i]	8	3	11
Total, mandatory spending included in core analysis [j]	1,834	130	1,964
Memorandum: All mandatory spending [k]	2,096	#N/A	#N/A
Selected discretionary programs			
Rental assistance [l]	34		
Special Supplemental Nutrition Program for Women, Infants, and Children	6		
Low Income Home Energy Assistance [n]	5		

Act with the goal of creating housing for poor and middle-income families in the nation. The text of the 1937 law read as follows:

> It is the policy of the United States (1) to promote the general welfare of the Nation by employing the funds and credit of the Nation ... (A) to assist States and political subdivisions of States to remedy the unsafe housing conditions and the acute shortage of decent and safe dwellings for low-income families; [and] (B) to assist States and political subdivisions of States to address the shortage of housing affordable to low-income families.[22]

The goal of this law was to improve the quality of housing for low- and medium-income people. It covered four basic areas of focus: demolition of substandard structures, revitalization of existing sites, replacement of current public housing options with better ones, and a tenant-based assistance grant program. The purpose of the law was articulated as follows:

(1) improving the living environment for public housing residents of severely distressed public housing projects through the demolition, rehabilitation,

reconfiguration, or replacement of obsolete public housing projects (or portions thereof);
(2) revitalizing sites (including remaining public housing dwelling units) on which such public housing projects are located and contributing to the improvement of the surrounding neighborhood;
(3) providing housing that will avoid or decrease the concentration of very low-income families; and
(4) building sustainable communities.[23]

The law required that for each new public housing unit created, a substandard housing unit must be removed. This law also gave local authorities the right of ownership and operation of the public housing units. This allowed localities to choose location and mode of operation for these public housing units. The national goals or objectives were clearly stated as building homes to benefit low- and moderate-income families, preventing the emergence of slums and blight, or aiding in their elimination, and meeting urgent community needs for housing.[24]

The law allowed local authorities who did not want public housing units to entirely avoid them. The result of this policy has been a high concentration of public housing units in low-income neighborhoods and a racialization of the public housing units to ethnic minorities. These factors have remained the character of public housing in most United States cities till today. In general, the focus of this program has been primarily capacity building for affordable housing and community development. This is done through different forms of block grants to communities, programs addressing homelessness, housing stability, and a variety of single-family housing programs that span from mortgage programs to insurance and rehabilitation mortgage insurance as well as multi-family housing programs.

Other poverty alleviation programs in the United States include the Children's Health Insurance Program, and the now controversial Affordable Care Act (or Obamacare). The Children's Health Insurance Program (CHIP) was created under President Bill Clinton in 1997 as part of the Balanced Budget Act of 1997. This program, a signature accomplishment of Hillary Clinton as First Lady, was aimed at addressing the more than ten million children in the United States in 1997 who were without medical coverage. The result of this program, as well as the expansion of Medicaid, led to a decline in the number of uninsured children in the United States from the ten million figure of 1997 to only 3.8 million in 2016.[25] The expansion of Medicaid as mentioned earlier began in 2014, with the passage of the Affordable Care Act.

The Affordable Care Act required state governments to expand Medicaid to extend to individuals under the age of sixty-five who come from families whose income level is below 133 percent of the Federal Poverty Level (FPL). The new law allowed for the newly eligible adults to be fully funded for Medicaid by the federal government for three years, and to phase down the coverage to 90 percent by the year 2020.[26] Sadly, this law is under a rigorous assault from the conservative right. The combined forces of a Republican Congress and a Republican White House are intent on doing away with this law and removing every vestige of the protections it offers to the poor.

CONCLUSION

The brevity of this chapter and the limitations of this book make it impossible to engage in a detailed discussion here of the problem of poverty in the United States. The same reason accounts for why the discussion has been limited to the United States and not expanded to include the global issues of poverty. A poll by the Gallup Organization asked people about their satisfaction level with their standard of living. The study showed that people who were dissatisfied with their income levels were also dissatisfied with their standard of living, meaning that there is nothing to romanticize about poverty. We must see it as a real problem that must be addressed in every society. It is also important to note that poverty is a trap.[27]

When one generation is living in poverty, the likelihood of the next generation being trapped in poverty is very high. So, poverty alleviation must never end with alleviation, but it must aim at the loftier goal of poverty eradication. If poverty can be stopped in one generation, it helps to prevent the next generation from falling into that trap.

This is where the power of free, fair, and equal education must be pursued as one of the many prongs for attacking the problem of poverty in the twenty-first century. Education remains the greatest social equalizer of all time. Multicultural education informs, empowers, and evens the playing field.

Notes

CHAPTER 1. FROM COLONIALISM TO A GLOBAL COMMUNITY

1. G. T. Stride & Caroline Ifeka, *People and Empires of West Africa: West Africa in History 1000–1800* (Edinburgh: Thomas Nelson and Sons Ltd., 1971).
2. Kevin Shillington, *History of Africa* (London: Palgrave Macmillan, 2012), 305.
3. Shillington, 2012, 304.
4. Kim Wale & Don Foster, "Investing in discourse of poverty and development: How white wealthy South Africans mobilize meaning to maintain privilege." *South African Review of Sociology* 38, no. 1 (2007): 50.
5. Cf. A. Bryant & S. B. Baker, "The feasibility of constructing profiles of Native Americans from the People of Color Racial Identity Attitude Scale: A brief report." *Measurement and Evaluation in Counseling and Development* 36, no. 1 (2003): 2–8.
6. W. Rowe, S. K. Bennett, & D. R. Atkinson, "White racial identity models: A critique and alternative proposal." *The Counseling Psychologist* 22, no. 1 (1994): 129–146; Kristen Heller, "Helm's white racial identity model." Last modified November 23, 2014. https://prezi.com/owhxtvs2yeed/helms-white-racial-identity-model/.
7. Zeus Leonardo, "The color of supremacy: Beyond the discourse of 'white privilege.'" *Educational Philosophy and Theory* 36, no. 2 (2004): 137–152.
8. Wale & Foster, 2007; M. Oliver, "The social construction of racial privilege in the United States: An asset perspective," in C. V. Hamilton, L. Huntley, N. Alexander, A. S. A. Guiaraes, & W. James (eds.), *Beyond Racism*, 251–272 (London: Lynne Rienner Publishers, 2001).
9. Leonardo, 2004, 141.
10. Cf. Sharlene Swartz, Emma Arogundade, & Danya Davis, "Unpacking (white) privilege in a South African university classroom: A neglected element in multicultural educational contexts." *Journal of Moral Education* 43, no. 3 (2014): 345–361.
11. David R. Paine, Peter J. Jankowski, & Steven J. Sandage, "Humility as a predictor of intercultural competence: Mediator effects for differentiation-of-self." *The*

Family Counseling Journal: Counseling and Therapy for Couples and Families 24, no. 1 (2016): 15–22.

12. Rowena Fong & Sharlene Furuto (eds.), *Culturally Competent Practice: Skills, Interventions, and Evaluations* (Boston: Allyn and Bacon, 2001); J. S. Gallegos, C. Tindall, & S. A. Gallegos, "The need for the advancement in conceptualization of cultural competence." *Advances in Social Work* 9, no. 1 (2008): 51–62; E. Lee, "Revisioning cultural competencies in clinical social work practice." *Families in Society* 91, no. 3 (2010): 272–279; Doman Lum, *Cultural Competence, Practice Stages and Client Systems: A Case Study Approach* (Belmont, CA: Thomson Brooks/Cole, 2004); Eleanor W. Lynch & Marci J. Hansen (eds.), *Developing Cross-Cultural Competencies: A Guide for Working with Children and Their Families*, 2nd ed. (Baltimore: Paul Brookes Publishing, 1998); Kimberleigh Nash & Jorge Velazquez Jr, *Cultural Competence: A Guide for Human Service Agencies*, rev. ed. (Washington, DC: Author, 2003); U.S. Department of Health and Human Services, *Cultural Competence Works: Using Cultural Competence to Improve the Quality of Health Care for Diverse Populations and Add Value to Managed Care Arrangement* (Merrifield, VA: Health Resources and Administration, 2001).

13. Milton Bennett, "A developmental approach to training for intercultural sensitivity." *International Journal of Intercultural Relations* 10, no. 2 (1986): 179–195; Milton Bennett, "Towards ethnorelativism: A developmental model of intercultural sensitivity," In M. Paige (ed.), *Education for the Intercultural Experience* (Yarmouth, ME: Intercultural Press, 1993); Milton Bennett, "Becoming interculturally competent," in J. Wurzel (ed.), *Toward Multiculturalism: A Reader in Multicultural Education*, 2nd ed., 62–77 (Newton, MA: Intercultural Resource, 2004); Milton Bennett, *Basic Concepts of Intercultural Communication: Paradigms, Principles, & Practices* (Boston: Intercultural Press, 2013).

14. Marcie Fisher-Borne, Jessie Montana Cain, & Suzanne L. Martin, "From mastery to accountability: Cultural humility as an alternative to cultural competence." *Social Work Education* 34, no. 2 (2015): 165–181.

15. Paine, Jankowski, & Sandage, 2016. Cf. Bolinger & Hill, 2012; Davis, Worthington, & Hook, 2010; Exline, 2012; Exline & Hill, 2012; Jankowski, Sandage, & Hill, 2013.

16. R. M. Ortega & K. C. Faller, "Training child welfare workers from an intersectional cultural perspective: A paradigm shift." *Child Welfare* 90, no. 5 (2011): 27–49.

17. Fisher-Borne et al., 2015.

18. Ortega & Faller, 2011.

19. T. R. Shannon, *An Introduction to the World-System Perspective* (New York: Westview Press, 1992).

20. A. Komlosy, M. Boatca, & H. Nolte, "Introduction: Coloniality of power and hegemonic shifts in the world-system." *Journal of World-Systems Research* 22, no. 2 (2016): 311.

21. Yash Tandon, "What is global apartheid and why do we fight it?" *Pambazuka News*, March 18, 2010. Accessed 09/27/18. https://www.pambazuka.org/global-south/what-global-apartheid-and-why-do-we-fight-it.

22. C. Chase-Dunn, "Five linked crises in the contemporary world-system." *American Psychological Association* 19, no. 2 (2013): 176.

23. Komlosy, Boatca, & Nolte, 2016.

24. W. A. Dunaway & D. A. Clelland, "Challenging the global apartheid model: A world-systems analysis." *Journal of World-Systems Research* 22, no. 1 (2016): 17.

25. Komlosy, Boatca, & Nolte, 2016.

CHAPTER 2. GLOBALIZATION AND MULTICULTURALISM

1. C. Cilliza, "The most important sentence President Obama uttered Tuesday." *Washington Post* July 23, 2014. Retrieved from https://www.washingtonpost.com/news/the-fix/wp/2014/07/23/the-most-important-sentence-president-obama-uttered-on-tuesday/.

2. J. S. Snider, S. Reysen, & I. Katzarska-Miller, "How we frame the message of globalization matters." *Journal of Applied Social Psychology* 43, no. 8 (2013): 1599–1607; B. Hamm, "Democracy in the light of globalization," in M. Mannermaa, J. Dator, & P. Tiihonen (eds.), *Democracy and Futures*, 100–112 (Helsinki, Finland: The Committee for the Future, 2006).

3. United Nations Population Fund, "Migration." 2017. Retrieved from http://www.unfpa.org/migration.

4. International Organization for Migration, "Global migration trends factsheet, 2015." Accessed 09/01/18. http://gmdac.iom.int/global-migration-trends-factsheet.

5. International Organization for Migration (IOM).

6. Phillip Connor, "International migration: Key findings from the U.S., Europe, and the world." Pew Research Center, December 15, 2016. Accessed 11/14/17.

7. International Organization for Migration (IOM).

8. Pew Research Center, "Origins and destinations of the world's migrants, from 1990–2015." Accessed 10/11/17. http://www.pewglobal.org/2016/05/17/global-migrant-stocks/?coiuntry=us&date=2015.

9. Philip G. Altbach, Liz Reisberg, & Laura E. Rumbley, "Tracking a global academic revolution." *Change: The Magazine of Higher Learning* 42, no. 2 (March/April 2010): 30–39.

10. New Media Consortium, *Horizon Report: Higher Education Edition* (Austin, TX: New Media Consortium, 2017).

11. A. J. Zurcher, "Citizenship," in Lauren S. Bahr & Bernard Johnston (eds.), *Collier's Encyclopedia*, 447 (New York: Macmillan Educational Company, 1992).

12. M. J. Pigozzi, "A UNESCO view of global citizenship education." *Educational Review* 58, no. 1 (2006): 1–4.

13. Y. Zhao, "A world at risk: An imperative for a paradigm shift to cultivate 21st century learners." *Society* 52, no. 2 (April 2015): 129–135.

14. R. J. Lieber & R. E. Weisberg, "Globalization, culture, and identities in crisis." *International Journal of Politics, Culture and Society* 16, no. 2 (2002): 273–296.

15. UN Division for Sustainable Development, "Transforming our world: The 2030 Agenda for Sustainable Development." 2015. Accessed 09/11/18. https://sustainabledevelopment.un.org/post 2015/transformingourworld.

16. J. Demaine, "Education and global citizenship: Strategies from below." *International Journal of Diversity* 5, no. 3 (2006): 103–109.

17. N. Fauzana, "The implication of globalization on education: Smart schools and values education." *International Journal of Diversity* 7, no. 2 (2007): 175.

18. A. Jochim & P. McGuinn, "The politics of the Common Core Assessments." *Education Next* 16, no. 4 (2016): 44–52.

19. Jochim & McGuinn, 2016.

20. Jochim & McGuinn, 2016.

21. S. L. Pense, B. W. Freeburg, & C. A. Clemons, "Implementation of Common Core State Standards: Choices, positions, and frames." *Career and Technical Education Research* 40, no. 3 (2015): 157–173.

22. Jochim & McGuinn, 2016.

23. P. E. Peterson, M. B. Henderson, M. R. West, & S. Barrows, "Common Core brand taints opinion on standards: 2016 findings and 10-year trends from the EdNext Poll." *Education Next* 17 no. 1 (2017): 8–28. Accessed 09/25/18. http://education next.org/ten-year-trends-in-public-opinion-from-ednext-poll-2016-survey/.

24. Jochim & McGuinn, 2016.

CHAPTER 3. FEDERAL AFFIRMATIVE ACTION AND ITS IMPLICATIONS FOR EQUAL EDUCATIONAL OPPORTUNITIES IN THE UNITED STATES

1. Ellen Berry, "Making civil rights claim for affirmative action." *Du Boise Review*, 12, no. 2 (2015): 375–405; P. Arcidiacono & M. Lovenheim, "Affirmative action and the quality-fit trade-off." *Journal of Economic Literature*, 54, no. 1 (2016): 3–51. doi:http://dx.doi.org/10.1257/jel.54.1.3.

2. B. K. Landsberg, *Affirmative Action: What is the law?* Paper presented at the California School Boards Association, Long Beach, CA, November 30 to December 3, 1995, p. 2.

3. U.S. Equal Employment Opportunities Commission. Title VII of the Civil Rights Act of 1964. Accessed 9/15/18. https://www.eeoc.gov/laws/statutes/titlevii.cfm; U.S. Department of Justice. Title VI of the Civil Rights Act of 1964 42 U.S.C. Accessed 09/25/18. https://www.justice.gov/crt/fcs/TitleVI-Overview.

4. U.S. Equal Employment Opportunities Commission.

5. Landsberg, 1995.

6. *University of California Regents v. Bakke* (1978), No. 76-811. Accessed 09/25/18. http://caselaw.findlaw.com/us-supreme-court/438/265.html.

7. Harvard Civil Rights Project, "Constitutional requirements for affirmative action in higher education admissions and financial aid." Paper from Research Roundtable: Affirmative Action in Higher Education and K–12, Cambridge, MA, 2001.

8. L. M. Garces & D. Mickey-Pabello, "Racial diversity in the medical profession: The impact of affirmative action bans on underrepresented student of color matriculation in medical schools." *The Journal of Higher Education* 86, no. 2 (2015): 254–294.

9. Garces & Mickey-Pabello, 2015.

10. Erin M. Hardtke, "Elimination of race as a factor in school admissions: An analysis of *Hopwood v. Texas*." *Marquette Law Review* 80, no. 4 (1997): 1135–1146. Accessed 6/17/18. http://scholarship.law.marquette.edu/mulr/vol80/iss4/7.

11. The Center for Individual Rights. *Hopwood v. Texas*, 1996. Accessed 7/15/16. https://www.cir-usa.org/cases/hopwood-v-texas/.

12. The Center for Individual Rights. *CIR's Historic Fifth Circuit Victory*. Accessed 7/14/17. https://www.cir-usa.org/cases.hopwood-v-texas/.

13. The Center for Individual Rights (CIR) describes itself as a nonprofit public interest law firm that is dedicated to the "defense" of individual liberties against the increasingly aggressive and unchecked authority of federal and state governments. It is a right wing advocacy group that is dedicated to enforcing constitutional limits on federal and state governments.

14. *Gratz v. Bolinger*, 123 S.Ct.2323, 2339, 2003.

15. M. R. Killenbeck, *Affirmative Action and Diversity: The Beginning of the End? Or the End of the Beginning?* (Princeton, NJ: Policy Information Center, 2004).

16. *Wooden v. NAACP*. Accessed 09/25/18. http://caselaw.findlaw.com/us-11th-circuit/1140908.html.

17. A. Springer, *Update on Affirmative Action in Higher Education: A Current Legal Overview* (Washington, DC: American Association of University Professors, 2003).

18. R. Plummer, "Black Brazil seeks a better future." *BBC News*, September 25, 2006. Accessed 11/14/17. http://newsvote.bbc.co.uk/mpapps/pagetools/print/news.bbc.co.uk/2/hi/americas/5357842.stm.

19. Debatepedia, "Position: Countries supporting affirmative action." Accessed 12/05/15. http://debatepedia.org/en/index.php/Position:Countries_supporting_affirmative_action.

20. J. Onsongo, "Affirmative action, gender equity and university admission—Kenya, Uganda, and Tanzania." *London Review of Education* 7, no. 1 (2009): 71–81.

21. L. Kearns, "High stakes standardized testing and marginalized youth: An examination of the impact on those who fail." *Canadian Journal of Education* 34 no. 2 (2011): 112–130; L. J. Schultz & J. C. Fortune, *The Three I's: Sources of Test Bias* (Washington, DC: Virginia Polytechnic Institute, 2001); C. Terrie, *Giving a Little Help to Girls? Evidence on Grade Discrimination and Its Effect on Students' Achievement* (London: Center for Economic Performance, 2005); J. Shannon, "Reading results: A critical look at standardized testing and the linguistic minority." Master of Science in Education degree thesis submitted to School of Education, Dominican University of California, 2008.

22. Association of American Medical Colleges, "MCAT scores and GPAs for applicants and matriculants to U.S. medical schools by race and ethnicity, Table 20919." Accessed April 24, 2018. https://www.aamc.org/download/321500/data/factstablea19.pdf; C. M. Steele, "A threat in the air: How stereotypes shape intellectual identity and performance." *American Psychologist* 52, no. 6 (1997): 613–629.

23. Garces & Mickey-Pabello, 2015.
24. Killenbeck, 2004.
25. Landsberg, 1995.
26. J. B. Slaughter, *After Michigan, What? Next Steps for Affirmative Action. Education Policy Institute, Policy Perspectives*. Accessed 09/12/18. www.educationalpolicy.org.
27. *Ballotpedia: The Encyclopedia of American Politics*. California Affirmative Action, Proposition 209 (1996). Accessed 09/09/18. https://ballotpedia.org/California_Affirmative_Action,_Proposition_209_(1996).
28. *Ballotpedia: The Encyclopedia of American Politics*, 1996.
29. P. Gandara, *California: A Case Study in the Loss of Affirmative Action. The Civil Rights Project/Proyoecto Derechos Civiles* (Los Angeles: The University of California, 2012).
30. L. M. Garces, *The Impact of Affirmative Action Bans in Graduate Education. The Civil Rights Project/Proyoecto Derechos Civiles* (Los Angeles: The University of California, 2012).
31. Colorado's Amendment 46 was aimed at ending affirmative action in the state of Colorado. Colorado voters voted to defeat the measure in November of 2008. More information on this measure and why it was defeated are available at the following source: Michele S. Moses, Amy Farley, Matthew Gaertner, Christina H. Paguyo, Darrell D. Jackson, & Kenneth R. Rowe, *Investigating the Defeat of Colorado's Amendment 46: An Analysis of the Trends and Principal Factors Influencing Voter Behaviors* (Boulder, CO: University of Colorado, 2010).
32. M. S. Moses, J. T. Yun, & P. Marin, "Affirmative Action's fate: Are 20 years more years enough?" *Education Policy Analysis Archives* 17, no. 17 (2009): 1–38.
33. T. J. Espenshade & C. Y. Chung, "The opportunity cost of admission preferences at elite universities." *Social Science Quarterly* 86, no. 2 (2005): 293–305.
34. E. Ashburn, "At elite colleges, legacy status may count more than was previously thought." *The Chronicle of Higher Education*, January 5, 2011. Accessed 6/23/18. http://chronicle.com/article/Legacys-Advantage-MayBe/125812/.

CHAPTER 4. GLOBAL ISSUES ON GENDER EQUITY

1. B. K. Herz & G. B. Sperling, *What Works in Girls' Education: Evidence and Policies from the Developing World* (New York: Council on Foreign Relations, 2004).
2. Reinie Cordier, Ben Milbourn, Robyn Martin, Angus Buchanan, Donna Chung, & Renée Speyer, "A systematic review evaluating the psychometric properties of measures of social inclusion." *PLoS One* 12, no. 6 (2017).
3. Aisha Ijaz & Tahir Abbas, "The impact of inter-generational change on the attitudes of working-class South Asian Muslim parents on the education of their daughters." *Gender and Education* 22, no. 3 (2010): 313–326.
4. Khalid Hossenini, *A Thousand Splendid Suns* (New York: Riverhead Books, 2007).

5. Jennifer L. Schenker, "The networked economy: How technology, innovation, and venture capital are transforming the future of mobile." *Informilo*, February 25–28, 2013. Accessed 10/12/16. http://www.informilo.com/wp-content/uploads/informilo_magazine_mwc_barcelona_march_2013.pdf.

6. T. M. Sheykhjan, K. Rajeswari, & K. Jabari, "Empowerment of women through education in the twenty-first century." Proceedings of the National Education Meet: Mapping new terrains for 21st century women, Nalanchira, Thiruvanthapram, Kerala, India, 2014.

7. I. Oplatka & O. Lapidot, "Muslim women in graduate studies: Some insights into the accessibility of higher education for minority women students." *Studies in Higher Education* 37, no. 3 (2012): 327–344.

8. C. L. Ryan & K. Bauman, "Educational attainment in the United States: 2015." Accessed 05/14/17. https://www.census.gov/content/dam/Census/library/publications/2016/demo/p20-578.pdf.

9. A. Latif, "A critical analysis of school enrollment and literacy rates of girls and women in Pakistan." *Educational Studies* 45, no. 5 (2009): 424–439.

10. Latif, 2009; Herz & Sperling, 2004.

11. N. Megahed & S. Lack, "Colonial legacy, women's rights and gender-educational inequality in the Arab world with particular reference to Egypt and Tunisia." *International Review of Education* 57, no. 3/4 (2011): 397–418.

12. Megahed & Lack, 2011.

13. World Economic Forum, *Global Gender Gap Report 2013* (Geneva, Switzerland: World Economic Forum, 2013).

14. A. J. Ifedili & C. A. Ifedili, "An evaluation of Beijing 1995 on the appointments and promotions of Nigerian women to decision-making positions." *Education* 130, no. 1 (2009): 118–128.

15. National Population Commission, *Nigeria Demographic and Education Survey, Adapted from Nigeria Demographic and Health Survey 2003* (Abuja, Nigeria: National Population Commission, 2004).

16. Megahed & Lack, 2011.

17. Latif, 2009, 426.

18. Ifedili & Ifedili, 2009.

19. Sheykhjan, Rajeswari, & Jabari, 2014, 45.

20. Sheykhjan, Rajeswari, & Jabari, 2014.

21. M. Ali & A. Ali, "Women's liberation through Islam: The freedom women gain from Islam." 2006. http://www.huda.tv/articles/women-in-islam/189-womens-liberation-through-islam.

22. Ali & Ali, 2005, 404.

23. N. Davids, "Muslim women and the politics of religious identity in a (post) secular society." *Studies in Philosophy and Education* 33, no. 3 (2014): 303–313.

24. B. F. Stowasser, *Women in the Qur'an, Traditions and Interpretations* (New York: Oxford University Press, 1994).

25. Megahed & Lack, 2011.

26. Megahed & Lack, 2011.

27. M. K. Evans, "Aba women's riot (November–December 1929)." Accessed 9/20/15. http://www.blackpast.org/gah/aba-women's-riot-november-december-1929; N. E. Mba, *Nigerian Women Mobilized: Women's Political Activity in Southern Nigeria 1900–1965* (Berkeley: University of California Press, 1982); L. L. Zukas, "Women's war of 1929." Revolution Protest Encyclopedia. Accessed 09/29/15. http://www.revolutionprotestencyclopedia.com/fragr_image/media/IEOWomens_War_of_1929.

28. D. Pearce, "The feminization of poverty: Women, work, and welfare." *The Urban & Social Change Review* 11, no. 1/2 (1978): 28–36; K. C. Sony, Bishnu Raj Upreti, & Bashu Prasad Subedi, "'We know the taste of sugar because of cardamom production': Links among commercial cardamom farming, women's involvement in production, and the feminization of poverty." *Journal of International Women's Studies* 18, no. 1 (2016): 181–207.

29. S. Fukundar-Parr, "What does feminization of poverty mean? It isn't just lack of income." *Feminist Economics* 5, no. 2 (1999): 99–103.

30. Schenker, 2013.

31. Eric Sylvers, "Mobilizing women: The industry is now focusing on closing the mobile gender gap." *Informilo*, February 25–28, 2013. Accessed 02/13/18. http://www.informilo.com/2013/02/mobilizing-women/.

32. J. K. Montz & A. Zajacova, "Why is life expectancy declining among low-educated women in the United States?" *American Journal of Public Health* 104, no. 10 (2014): e5–e7.

33. K. Running & L. M. Roth, "To wed or work? Assessing work and marriage as routes out of poverty." *Journal of Poverty* 17, no. 2 (2013): 177–197.

34. M. Thibos, D. Lavin-Loucks, & M. Martin, "The feminization of poverty." A report prepared for the 2007 Joint Policy Forum on the Feminization of Poverty sponsored by The William Institute and the YWCA, May 7, 2007.

35. J. Rubery & A. Rafferty, "Women and recession revisited." *Work, Employment and Society* 27, no. 3 (2013): 414–432. doi:10.1177/0950017012460314.

36. Rubery & Rafferty, 2013.

37. S. Trygged, E. Hedlund, & I. Kareholt, "Beaten and poor? A study of the long-term economic situation of women victims of severe violence." *Social Work in Public Health* 29, no. 2 (2014): 100–113.

38. A. Belzunegui, O. Matu, & I. Pastor, "Gender and poverty in Spain." *Revista Romana de Sociologie* 24, no. 1/2 (2013): 75–89.

39. Y. Batana, "Multidimensional measurement of poverty among women in sub-Saharan Africa." *Social Indicators Research* 112, no. 2 (2013): 337–362.

40. L. Akpor, "Trafficking of women in Nigeria: Causes, consequences and the way forward." *Corvinus Journal of Sociology and Social Policy* 2, no. 2 (2011): 89–110.

41. T. Fadaak, "Poverty in the kingdom of Saudi Arabia: An exploratory study of poverty and female-headed households in Jeddah City." *Social Policy & Administration* 44, no. 6 (2010): 689–707.

42. A. Mohammadpur, J. Karimi, & M. Alizadeh, "Women and culture of poverty (a qualitative study of the culture of poverty among the Iranian caretaker women)." *Quality and Quantity* 48, no. 1 (2014): 1–14.

43. L. Zhibin, "Chinese women and poverty alleviation: Reflections and prospects for the future." *Chinese Sociology and Anthropology* 40, no. 4 (2008): 27–37.

44. S. M. Hassan & K. Ahmad, "Globalization: Feminization of poverty and need for gender responsive social protection in Pakistan." *Pakistan Vision* 15, no. 2 (2014): 58–80.

45. J. Ward, C. Turner, J. Watts, & J. Eldred, "Every woman's right to learn." *Adult Learning* 22, no. 6 (2011): 12–13.

46. United Nations. Convention on the Political Rights of Women. *Chapter XVI. Status of Women.* New York, United Nations: 1953.

47. United Nations. Convention on the Nationality of Married Women. *Chapter XVI. Status of Women.* New York: United Nations, 1957.

48. United Nations. Convention on Consent to Marriage, Minimum Age for Marriage and Registration of Marriage. Resolution Adopted by the General Assembly of the United Nations 1763 A (XVII), November 7, 1962.

49. United Nations. Resolution Adopted by the General Assembly 3520 (XXX). World Conference of the International Women's Year. Thirtieth Session, Agenda item 75. New York, 1975.

50. United Nations, 1975.

51. United Nations, 1975; United Nations. United Nations Decade for Women. Resolution Adopted by the General Assembly 31/136. Thirty-First Session, Agenda item 75. New York; 1976.

52. United Nations. Convention on the Elimination of All Forms of Discrimination against Women. Resolution Adopted by the United Nations General Assembly 2263 (XXII), Twenty-Second Session. New York, United Nations, 1979.

53. United Nations, 1979.

54. D. Bernard, "The Synergy of 'Rights' Conventions: The Convention on the Elimination of All Forms of Discrimination Against Women (CEDAW), the Convention on the Rights of the Child (CRC), the Inter-American Convention on the Prevention, Punishment and Eradication of Violence Against Women (The Convention of Belem do Para)." Paper presented at the Caribbean Conference on the Rights of the Child: Meeting the Post-Ratification Challenge, Belize City, Belize, October 7–10, 1996.

55. United Nations. Declaration on the Elimination of Violence against Women, 1993, Article 1. Accessed 09/12/18. http://www.un.org/documents/ga/res/48/a48r104.htm.

56. United Nations. Beijing Declaration and Platform for Action. New York: United Nations, 1995.

57. Catalyst, *Catalyst Quick Take: Women's Earnings and Income* (New York: Catalyst, 2015).

58. World Health Organization, "Violence against women: Intimate partner and sexual violence against women." WHO, November 29, 2017. Accessed 10/7/15 from http://www.who.int/mediacentre/factsheets/fs239/en/.

59. World Health Organization, "Global Health Observatory (GHO) data." Accessed 10/7/15. https://www.who.int/gho/en/.

60. Illinois Department of Public Health, "Facts about violence against women." Accessed 9/26/15 from http://www.idph.state.il.us/about/womenshealth/factsheets/viol.htm.

61. National Coalition for Women and Girls in Education. *Title IX at 35*. Washington, DC: National Coalition for Women and Girls in Education, 2008.

62. P. Tjaden & N. Thoennes, *Full Report of the Prevalence, Incidence, and Consequences of Violence against Women* (Washington, DC: National Institute of Justice, Office of Justice Programs, U.S. Department of Justice, and the Centers for Disease Control and Prevention, 2000).

63. Rape, Abuse & Incest National Network, "Victims of sexual violence: Statistics." https://www.rainn.org/statistics/victims-sexual-violence.

64. P. Kime, "Incidents of rape in military much higher than previously reported." *Military Times*, December 4, 2014. Accessed 9/26/15. https://www.militarytimes.com/2014/12/04/incidents-of-rape-in-military-much-higher-than-previously-reported/.

65. United Nations, *Shame of War: Sexual Violence against Women and Girls in Conflict* (Nairobi: United Nations Office for the Coordination of Humanitarian Affairs Integrated Regional Information Network, 2007).

CHAPTER 5. THE ADVANCEMENT OF GENDER EQUITY IN THE UNITED STATES

1. K. J. Maxwell, "League of Women Voters through the decades!" League of Women Voters of the United States, 2007. Accessed October 6, 2015 from http://lwv.org/contents/league-women-voters-through-decades.

2. Maxwell, 2007.

3. National Council of Negro Women, Inc., "History." Accessed 10/6/2015. https://www.lwv.org/about-us/history.

4. Equal Employment Opportunity Commission, 1947. The Equal Pay Act of 1963; Equal Employment Opportunity Commission. (1964). Title VII of the Civil Rights Act of 1964. United States of America Congress. Section 2000e, Pub. L. 88-352.

5. Equal Employment Opportunity Commission, 1947.

6. C. F. Epstein, "Reflections on women and the law in the USA." *International Social Science Journal* 59, no. 191 (2009): 17–26.

7. Encyclopedia.com, "National Organization for Women." Accessed 9/12/16. http://www.encyclopedia.com/topic/National_Organization_for_Women.aspx.

8. Encyclopedia.com, 2016.

9. Encyclopedia.com, 2016.

10. Epstein, 2009.

11. *Encyclopaedia Britannica*. National Women's Political Caucus (NWPC). Accessed 3/13/16. https://www.britannica.com/topic/National-Womens-Political-Caucus.

12. United States Department of Justice. Overview of Title IX of the Education Amendment of 1972, U.S.C. A§ 1681 ET. SEQ. Accessed 09/25/18. https://www.justice.gov/crt/overview-title-ix-education-amendments-1972-20-usc-1681-et-seq; United States Department of Labor. (2016). Title IX, Education Amendment of 1972. Retrieved from https://www.dol.gov/oasam/regs/statutes/titleix.htm.

13. I. Valentin, *Title IX: A Brief History. 25 Years of Title IX*. WEEA Digest (Newton, MA: WEEA Equity Resource Center at EDC, 1997).

R. Lapchick, J. Fox, A. Guiao, & M. Simpson, *The 2014 Racial and Gender Report Card: College Sport* (Orlando: The Institute for Diversity and Ethics in Sport, 2015).

15. National Association of Working Women, "Our story." 2015. Accessed 10/6/2015. http://9to5.org/about-u/our-story/.
16. United States General Accounting Office. Women's Educational Equity Act. A Review of Program Goals and Strategies Needed. *Report to Congressional Requesters*, December 1994, 28.
17. United States Department of Education. *Report to the White House Council on Women and Girls*. U.S. Department of Education Agency Report, July 6, 2010.
18. Feminist Majority Foundation. *History of Feminist Majority Foundation*. Arlington, VA: Feminist Majority Foundation, 2014.
19. J. Warner, *The Women's Leadership Gap* (Washington DC: Center for American Progress, May 27, 2017). Accessed 09/27/18. https://www.americanprogress.org/issues/women/reports/2017/05/21/432758/womens-leadership-gap/.
20. National Center for Education Statistics. (2006). *Digest of Education Statistics: 2005*. Washington DC: U.S. Department of Education, Institute of Education Sciences; College Board. (2006). AP Summary Report. Downloaded October 7, 2015 from http://www.collegeboard.com/student/testing/ap/exgrd_sum/2006.html; 66th Annual Intel Science Talent Search (2006–2007). (2007). Finalists, Science Service. January 2007; National Science Foundation. (2004). Women, Minorities, and Persons with Disabilities in Science and Engineering: 2004. Arlington, VA: National Science Foundation, Division of Science Resources Statistics.
21. Bureau of Labor Statistics. United States Department of Labor, Women's Bureau: Latest Annual Data (2013). Accessed 9/19/18. http://www.bls.gov/cps/cpsaat03.htm.
22. National Coalition for Women and Girls in Education (NCWGE), *Title IX at 30: Report Card on Gender Equity* (Washington, DC: National Coalition for Women and Girls in Education, 2002).
23. National Coalition for Women and Girls in Education (NCWGE), *Title IX at 35* (Washington, DC: National Coalition for Women and Girls in Education, 2008).
24. B. H. Wootton, "Gender differences in occupational employment." *Monthly Labor Review* 120, no. 4 (April 1997): 15–24; Kimberlee A. Shauman, "Gender differences in the early employment outcomes of STEM doctorates." *Social Sciences* 6, no. 1 (2017): 24.
25. United States Department of Labor. Latest Annual Data. United States Department of Labor, Women's Bureau. Accessed 10/7/15 from http://www.dol.gov/wb/stats/stats_data.htm.
26. American Association of University Women, *The Simple Truth about the Gender Pay Gap* (Washington, DC: AAUW, 2014); Kristen Roche, "Millennials and the gender wage gap in the U.S.: A cross-cohort comparison of young workers born in the 1960s and the 1980s." *Atlantic Economic Journal* 45, no. 3 (2017): 333–350.
27. Catalyst, *Catalyst Quick Take: Women's Earnings and Income* (New York: Catalyst, 2015).
28. Ariane Hegewisch, Emily Ellis, & Heidi Hartmann, "The gender wage gap: 2014; Earnings differences by race and ethnicity." Institute of Women's Policy Research, March 6, 2014. Accessed 10/7/15. https://iwpr.org/publications/the-gender-wage-gap-2014-earnings-differences-by-race-and-ethnicity/.

CHAPTER 6. RELIGIOUS DIVERSITY AND THE PUBLIC SCHOOL SYSTEMS

1. C. N. Quigley, *Constitutional Democracy* (Calabasas, CA: Center for Civic Education, n.d.); B. Mohamed, "New estimates show U.S. Muslim population continues to grow" (Washington, DC: Pew Research Center, 2018). Retrieved from http://www.pewresearch.org/fact-tank/2018/01/03/new-estimates-show-u-s-muslim-population-continues-to-grow/.

2. The First Amendment to the US Constitution.

3. "*Reynolds v. United States*." Oyez.org. Accessed June 19, 2018. https://www.oyez.org/cases/1850-1900/98us145.

4. "*Reynolds v. United States*." Berkeley Center for Religion, Peace, and World Affairs. Accessed June 7, 2018. https://berkleycenter.georgetown.edu/cases/reynolds-v-united-states.

5. "*Abington School District v. Schemp*." Findlaw..com. Accessed June 7, 2018. https://caselaw.findlaw.com/us-supreme-court/374/203.html.

6. "*School District of Abington Township, Pennsylvania v. Schempp*." Oyez.org. Accessed June 19, 2018. https://www.oyez.org/cases/1962/142.

7. Guidance on Constitutionally Protected Prayer in Public Elementary and Secondary Schools, February 7, 2003. US Department of Education. Accessed June 14, 2018. http://www.ed.gov/policy/gen/guid/religionandschools/prayer_guidance.html.

8. William Jefferson Clinton was the 42nd US president, serving as president from 1993 to 2001. His administration's position on prayer in schools is accessible at http://www.ed.gov/policy/gen/guid/religionandschools/prayer_guidance.html.

9. C. Riley, "Religious expression in public schools." Archived information, United States Department of Education. *The Secretary*, 1998. Accessed June 15, 2018. http://www.ed.gov/policy/gen/guid/religionandschools/prayer_guidance.html.

10. Cf. http://www.ed.gov/policy/gen/guid/religionandschools/prayer_guidance.html.

11. Riley, 1998.

12. Pew Research Center, "America's changing religious landscape." Pew Research Center, Demographic Study, May 12, 2015. Retrieved from http://www.pewforum.org/2015/05/12/americas-changing-religious-landscape/.

13. K. I. Hossain, "Understanding Islam in the U.S. classroom: A guide for elementary school teachers." *Multicultural Education* 20, no. 2 (2013): 49–52.

14. S. Niyozov, "Teachers and teaching Islam and Muslims in pluralistic societies: Claims, misunderstandings, and responses." *Journal of International Migration & Integration* 11, no. 1 (2010): 23–40.

15. Hossain, 2013, 49–52.

16. Thomas Reuters. *Zorach v. Clauson*, 1952. Accessed 06/15/18. https://caselaw.findlaw.com/us-supreme-court/343/306.html.

17. *McCollum v. Board of Education*, 333 U.S. 203 (1948). Justia.com. Accessed June 19, 2018. https://supreme.justia.com/cases/federal/us/333/203/case.html.

18. "*Engel v. Vitale*." Oyez.org. Accessed June 19, 2018. https://www.oyez.org/cases/1961/468.

19. "*Engel v. Vitale.*" United States Courts. Accessed June 19, 2018. http://www.uscourts.gov/educational-resources/educational-activities/facts-and-case-summary-engel-v-vitale.
20. "*Engel v. Vitale.*" Oyez.org. Accessed June 19, 2018. https://www.oyez.org/cases/1961/468.
21. John E. Taylor, "30 years after *Edwards v. Aguillard*: Why creationism lingers in public schools." *The Conversation*, 2017. Accessed June 19, 2018. http://the conversation.com/30-years-after-edwards-v-aguillard-why-creationism-lingers-in-public-schools-79603.
22. "*Edwards v. Aguillard.*" Legal Information Institute. Accessed June 19, 2018. https://www.law.cornell.edu/supremecourt/text/482/578.
23. "*Edwards v. Aguillard.*" Oyez.org. Accessed June 19, 2018. https://www.oyez.org/cases/1986/85-1513.
24. Taylor, 2017.

CHAPTER 7. THE CHALLENGE OF POVERTY IN TWENTY-FIRST-CENTURY AMERICA

1. NURU International. Extreme Poverty. Accessed June 23, 2018. http://www.nuruinternational.org/why/extreme-poverty/; UN-DEAS Division for sustainable Development Goals. (2017). Sustainable Development Goal 1: End poverty in all its forms everywhere. Retrieved from https://sustainabledevelopment.un.org/sdg1.
2. MPH@GW. (2018). Poverty vs. Federal Poverty Level. Accessed June 23, 2018. https://publichealthonline.gwu.edu/blog/poverty-vs-federal-poverty-level/.
3. OPHI. (n.d.). Policy—A multidimensional approach. Accessed June 23, 2018. https://ophi.org.uk/policy/multidimensional-poverty-index/.
4. S. Alkire & G. Robles, "Multidimensional poverty index summer 2017: Brief methodological note and results." *OPHI Methodological Note* 44, 2017. University of Oxford. Accessed June 23, 2018. https://ophi.org.uk/multidimensional-poverty-index/global-mpi-2017/.
5. Susan McFarland, "U.N. report: With 40M in poverty, U.S. most unequal developed nation." *UPI*, 2018. Accessed June 23, 2018. https://www.upi.com/UN-report-With-40M-in-poverty-US-most-unequal-developed-nation/8671529664548/.
6. Linda Kinkade, "America's poor becoming more destitute under Trump, UN report says." *CNN*, 2018. Accessed June 23, 2018. https://www.cnn.com/2018/06/22/us/america-poverty-un-report/index.html.
7. Bernard Dryer, Paul J. Chung, P. Szilagyi, & Shale Wong, "Child poverty in the United States today: Introduction and executive summary." *Academic Pediatrics* 16, no. 3 (2016): s1–s5. https://doi.org/10.1016/j.acap.2016.02.010.
8. McFarland, 2018.
9. MPH@GW, 2018.
10. UNICEF, "Children bear the brunt of poverty." UNICEF.org, 2017. Accessed June 23, 2018. http://data.unicef.org/topic/overview/child-poverty/#.

11. UNICEF, "Ending extreme poverty: A focus on children." UNICEF.org, 2016. Accessed June 23, 2018. http://data.unicef.org/wp-content/uploads/2017/09/Ending_Extreme_Poverty_A_Focus_on_Children_Oct_2016.pdf.

12. Amanda Lee, "U.S. poverty thresholds and poverty guidelines: What's the difference?" PRB.org, 2018. Accessed June 23, 2018. https://www.prb.org/insight/u-s-poverty-thresholds-and-poverty-guidelines-whats-the-difference/.

13. NCPP, "Child poverty." NCPP.org, 2018. Accessed June 23, 2018. http://www.nccp.org/topics/childpoverty.html.

14. NCPP, "Children's mental health." NCPP.org, 2018. Accessed June 23, 2018. http://www.nccp.org/topics/mentalhealth.html.

15. World Health Organization. Millennium Development Goals (MDGs). Retrieved from http://www.who.int/topics/millennium_development_goals/about/en/.

16. United Nations. (1995). Report of the World Summit for Social Development. Retrieved from https://www.un.org/documents/ga/conf166/aconf166-9.htm.

17. United Nations, 1995.

18. D. Belland & A. Waddan, "Why are there no universal social programs in the United States? A historical institutionalist comparison with Canada." *World Affairs* 180, no. 1 (2017): 64–92.

19. Belland & Waddan, 2017.

20. C. Lin & M. Lee, "A comparative policy analysis of family preservation programs in the U.S. and in Taiwan." *Journal of Child and Family Studies* 25, no. 4 (2015): 1131–1144.

21. *The Nation*, "151 years of America's housing history." TheNation.com, 2018. Accessed 08/12/18. https://www.thenation.com/article/americas-housing-history/.

22. United States Housing Act of 1937. Retrieved from http://www.bostonfairhousing.org/timeline/1937-Housing-Act.html; The Fair Housing Center of Greater Boston. (n.d.); 1937: The Housing Act (Wagner-Steagall Act). Accessed 09/27/18. http://www.bostonfairhousing.org/timeline/1937-Housing-Act.html.

23. HUD. US Housing Act of 1947, as amended. Accessed 7/12/18. https://www.hud.gov/sites/documents/DOC_10010.PDF.

24. U.S. Department of Housing and Urban Development. *Programs of HUD*. Washington DC: U.S. Department of Housing and Urban Development, 2017.

25. The Medicaid and CHIP Payment and Access Commission. (2018). History and impact of CHIP. Accessed 08/12/18. https://www.macpac.gov/subtopic/history-and-impact-of-chip/.

26. Centers for Medicare & Medicaid Services. Program History. Accessed 08/02/18. https://www.medicaid.gov/about-us/program-history/index.html.

27. M. Roser & E. Ortiz-Ospina, "Global extreme poverty." OurWorldInData.org, 2013. Accessed 07/12/17. https://ourworldindata.org/extreme-poverty; Justin McCarthy, "Americans' assessments of living standards brighter in 2015 (January 6, 2016)." Gallup.com, 2016. https://news.gallup.com/poll/188048/americans-assessments-living-standards-brighter015.aspx?g_source=link_NEWSV9&g_medium=TOPIC&g_campaign=item_&g_content=Americans%27%2520Assessments%2520of%2520Living%2520Standards%2520Brighter%2520in%25202015.

References

A&E Television Networks, LLC. "Civil Rights Act of 1964." https://www.history.com/topics/black-history/civil-rights-act.

Abington School District v. Schemp, U.S. Supreme Court, 374 U.S. 203. Findlaw.com. https://caselaw.findlaw.com/us-supreme-court/374/203.html.

Akpor, L. "Trafficking of women in Nigeria: Causes, consequences and the way forward." *Corvinus Journal of Sociology and Social Policy* 2, no. 2 (2011): 89–110.

Altbach, Philip G., Liz Reisberg, & Laura E. Rumbley. "Tracking a global academic revolution." *Change: The Magazine of Higher Learning* 42 no. 2 (2010): 30–39.

Ali, M., & A. Ali. "Women's liberation through Islam: The freedom women gain from Islam." 2006. http://www.huda.tv/articles/women-in-islam/189-womens-liberation-through-islam.

Alkire, S., & G. Robles. "Multidimensional poverty index, summer 2017: Brief methodological note and results." *OPHI Methodological Note 44*, 2017. University of Oxford. https://ophi.org.uk/multidimensional-poverty-index/global-mpi-2017/.

Allen, A., & C. Stegmeir. *Civics*. New York: American Book Company, 1956.

American Association of University Women. *The Simple Truth about the Gender Pay Gap*. Washington, DC: AAUW, 2014.

Arcidiacono, P., & M. Lovenheim. "Affirmative action and the quality-fit trade-off." *Journal of Economic Literature* 54, no. 1 (2016): 3–51. doi:http://dx.doi.org/10.1257/jel.54.1.3.

Ashburn, E. "At elite colleges, legacy status may count more than was previously thought." *The Chronicle of Higher Education*, January 5, 2011. http://chronicle.com/article/Legacys-Advantage-MayBe/125812/.

Association of American Medical Colleges. "MCAT scores and GPAs for applicants and matriculants to U.S. medical schools by race and ethnicity, Table 20919," 2012. AAMC.org. https://www.aamc.org/download/321500/data/factstablea19.pdf.

Ballotpedia: The Encyclopedia of American Politics, California Affirmative Action, Proposition 209 (1996). https://ballotpedia.org/California_Affirmative_Action,_Proposition_209_(1996).

Batana, Y. "Multidimensional measurement of poverty among women in sub-Saharan Africa." *Social Indicators Research* 112, no. 2 (2013): 337–362.

Barba, R. H. *Science in the Multicultural Classroom.* Boston: Allyn and Bacon, 1998.

Barr, L. "The next step: Showing a common history of treatment for minorities, women and gays in media content, newsrooms and journalism schools: A proposal for future research and suggestions for a curriculum." A paper presented at the 76th annual meeting of the Association for Education in Journalism and Mass Communication, Kansas City, MO, August 11–14, 1993.

Batana, Y. "Multidimensional measurement of poverty among women in sub-Saharan Africa." *Social Indicators Research* 112, no. 2 (2013): 337–362.

Beisel, N., & T. Kay. "Abortion, race, and gender in nineteenth-century America." *American Sociological Review*, 69, no. 4 (2004): 498–518.

Belland, D., & A. Waddan. "Why are there no universal social programs in the United States? A historical institutionalist comparison with Canada." *World Affairs* 180, no. 1 (2017): 64–92.

Belzunegui, A., O. Matu, & I. Pastor, "Gender and poverty in Spain." *Revista Romana de Sociologie* 24, no. 1/2 (2013): 75–89.

Bennett, Milton. "A developmental approach to training for intercultural sensitivity." *International Journal of Intercultural Relations* 10, no. 2 (1986): 179–195.

Bennett, Milton. *Basic Concepts of Intercultural Communication: Paradigms, Principles, & Practices.* Boston: Intercultural Press, 2013.

Bennett, Milton. "Becoming interculturally competent." In J. Wurzel (ed.), *Toward Multiculturalism: A Reader In Multicultural Education.* 2nd ed. Newton, MA: Intercultural Resource, 2004.

Bennett, Milton. "Towards ethnorelativism: A developmental model of intercultural sensitivity." In M. Paige (ed.), *Education for the Intercultural Experience.* Yarmouth, ME: Intercultural Press, 1993.

Bernard, D. "The Synergy of 'Rights' Conventions: The Convention on the Elimination of All Forms of Discrimination Against Women (CEDAW), the Convention on the Rights of the Child (CRC), the Inter-American Convention on the Prevention, Punishment and Eradication of Violence Against Women (The Convention of Belem do Para)." Paper presented at the Caribbean Conference on the Rights of the Child: Meeting the Post-Ratification Challenge, Belize City, Belize, October 7–10, 1996.

Berry, Ellen. "Making civil rights claim for affirmative action." *Du Boise Review* 12, no. 2 (2015): 375–405.

Bollinger, R. A., & P. C. Hill. "Humility." In T. G. Plante (ed.), *Religion, Spirituality, and Positive Psychology: Understanding the Psychological Fruits of Faith.* Santa Barbara, CA: Praeger, 2012.

Brown v. Board of Education, 347 U.S. 483 (1954) (USSC+). Supreme Court of the United States.

Bryant, A., & S. B. Baker. "The feasibility of constructing profiles of Native Americans from the People of Color Racial Identity Attitude Scale: A brief report." *Measurement and Evaluation in Counseling and Development* 36, no. 1 (2003): 2–8.

Bureau of Labor Statistics. *United States Department of Labor, Women's Bureau: Latest Annual Data, 2013.* http://www.bls.gov/cps/cpsaat03.htm.

California Department of Education. *Improving Academic Achievement*, 2016. http://www.cde.ca.gov/sp/sw/t1/.

Catalyst. *Catalyst Quick Take: Women's Earnings and Income.* New York: Catalyst, 2015.

The Center for Individual Rights. *Hopwood v. Texas*, 1996. https://www.cir-usa.org/cases/hopwood-v-texas/.

The Center for Individual Rights. "CIR's historic fifth circuit victory." https://www.cir-usa.org/cases.hopwood-v-texas/.

Centers for Medicare & Medicaid Services. "Program history." https://www.medicaid.gov/about-us/program-history/index.html.

Chase-Dunn, C. "Five linked crises in the contemporary world-system." *American Psychological Association* 19, no. 1 (2013): 175–180.

Cilliza, C. "The most important sentence President Obama uttered Tuesday." *Washington Post*, July 23, 2014. https://www.washingtonpost.com/news/the-fix/wp/2014/07/23/the-most-important-sentence-president-obama-uttered-on-tuesday/.

Coates, T. *Between the World and Me.* New York: Spiegel & Grau, 2015.

College Board. *AP Summary Report*, 2006. http://www.collegeboard.com/student/testing/ap/exgrd_sum/2006.html.

Committee on Education Funding. "Programs in the ESEA Framework (Every Student Succeeds Act) as approved by the Conference Committee: All programs are authorized from FY 2017 through FY (All numbers in thousands)." 2016. https://www.aasa.org/uploadedFiles/Policy_and_Advocacy/files/PROGRAMS%20IN%20THE%20ESEA%20FRAMEWORK.pdf.

Common Core State Standards Initiative. "Development process." http://www.corestandards.org/about-the-standards/development-process/.

Connor, Phillip. "International migration: Key findings from the U.S., Europe and the world." Pew Research Center, December 15, 2016. http://www.pewresearch.org/facttank/2016/12/15/international-migrant-key-findings-from-the-u-s-europe-and-the-world/.

Cordier, Reinie, Ben Milbourn, Robyn Martin, Angus Buchanan, Donna Chung, & Renée Speyer. "A systematic review evaluating the psychometric properties of measures of social inclusion." *PLoS One* 12, no. 6 (2017).

Council on American-Islamic Relations. *An Educator's Guide to Islamic Religious Practices.* Washington, DC: Council on American-Islamic Relations, 2005.

Davids, N. "Muslim women and the politics of religious identity in a (post)secular society." *Studies in Philosophy and Education* 33, no. 3 (2014): 303–313.

Davis, D. E., E. L. Worthington Jr., & J. N. Hook. "Humility: Review of measurement strategies and conceptualization as personal judgment." *Journal of Positive Psychology* 5 (2010): 243–252.

Davy, B., U. Davy, & L. Leisering. "The global, the social, and rights: New perspectives on social citizenship." *International Journal of Social Welfare* 22 (2013): S1–S14.

Debatepedia. "Position: Countries supporting affirmative action." http://debatepedia.org/en/index.php/Position:Countries_supporting_affirmative_action.

The Declaration of Independence, 1776. http://members.tripod.com~candst/thompson.htm.

Demaine, J. "Education and global citizenship: Strategies from below." *International Journal of Diversity* 5, no. 3 (2006): 103–109.

Dermott, E., & C. Pantazis. "Gender and poverty in Britain: Changes and continuities between 1999 and 2012." *Journal of Poverty and Social Justice* 22, no. 3 (2014): 253–269.

Dever, M., M. Whitaker, & D. Brynes. "The 4th R: Teaching about religion in the public schools." *Social Studies* 92 (2001): 220–229.

Dryer, Bernard, Paul J. Chung, P. Szilagyi, & Shale Wong, "Child poverty in the United States today: Introduction and executive summary." *Academic Pediatrics* 16, no. 3 (2016): s1–s5. https://doi.org/10.1016/j.acap.2016.02.010.

Du Bois, W. E. B. *Black Reconstruction*. New York: Harcourt Brace, 1935.

Dunaway, W. A., & D. A. Clelland. "Challenging the global apartheid model: A world-systems analysis." *Journal of World-Systems Research* 22, no. 1 (2016): 16–22.

Dunlap, M., J. Scoggin, P. Green, & A. Davi. "White students' experiences of privilege and socioeconomic disparities: Towards a theoretical model." *Michigan Journal of Community Service Learning* (2007): 19–30.

"*Edwards v. Aguillard*." Legal Information Institute. https://www.law.cornell.edu/supremecourt/text/482/578.

"*Edwards v. Aguillard*." Oyez.org. https://www.oyez.org/cases/1986/85-1513.

"Elimination of race as a factor in school admissions: An analysis of *Hopwood v. Texas*." 2015. http://scholarship.law.marquette.edu/cgi/viewcontent.gi?article=1518&context=mulr.

Ellis, P. H. "White racial identity development at a two-year institute." *Community College Journal of Research and Practice* 28 (2002): 745–761.

Encyclopaedia Britannica. "National Women's Political Caucus (NWPC)." https://www.britannica.com/topic/National-Womens-Political-Caucus.

Encyclopedia.com. "National Organization for Women." http://www.encyclopedia.com/topic/National_Organization_for_Women.aspx.

"*Engel v. Vitale*." Justia.com. https://supreme.justia.com/cases/federal/us/370/421/.

"*Engel v. Vitale*." Oyez.org. https://www.oyez.org/cases/1961/468.

"*Engel v. Vitale*." United States Courts. http://www.uscourts.gov/educational-resources/educational-activities/facts-and-case-summary-engel-v-vitale.

Epstein, C. F. "Reflections on women and the law in the USA." *International Social Science Journal* 59, no. 191 (2009): 17–26.

Espenshade, T. J., & C. Y. Chung, "The opportunity cost of admission preferences at elite universities." *Social Science Quarterly* 86, no. 2 (2005): 293–305.

Equal Employment Opportunity Commission. (1964). Title VII of the Civil Rights Act of 1964. United States of America Congress. Section 2000e, Pub. L. 88-352.

Equal Employment Opportunity Commission. (1947). The Equal Pay Act of 1963.

Evans, M. K. "Aba women's riot (November–December 1929)." http://www.blackpast.org/gah/aba-women's-riot-november-december-1929.

Exline, J. J., & P. C. Hill. (2012). "Humility: A consistent and robust predictor of generosity." *Journal of Positive Psychology* 7 (2012): 208–218.

Exline, J. J. "Humility and the ability to receive from others." *Journal of Psychology and Christianity* 31 (2012): 182–191.

Fadaak, T. "Poverty in the kingdom of Saudi Arabia: An exploratory study of poverty and female-headed households in Jeddah City." *Social Policy & Administration* 44, no. 6 (2010): 689–707.

The Fair Housing Center of Greater Boston. "1937: The Housing Act (Wagner-Steagall Act)," n.d. http://www.bostonfairhousing.org/timeline/1937-Housing-Act.html.

Faist, T. "The transnational social question: Social rights and citizenship in a global context." *International Sociology* 24, no. 1 (2009): 7–35.

The Fair Housing Center of Greater Boston. "1937: The Housing Act (Wagner-Steagall Act)," n.d. http://www.bostonfairhousing.org/timeline/1937-Housing-Act.html.

Fauzana, N. "The implication of globalization on education: Smart schools and values education." *International Journal of Diversity* 7, no. 2 (2007): 175.

Feminist Majority Foundation. *History of Feminist Majority Foundation*. Arlington, VA: Feminist Majority Foundation, 2014.

Fisher-Borne, M., J. M. Cain, & S. L. Martin. "From mastery to accountability: Cultural humility as an alternative to cultural competence." *Social Work Education* 34, no. 2 (2015): 165–181.

Fong, R., & S. Furuto (eds.). *Culturally Competent Practice: Skills, Interventions, and Evaluations*. Boston: Allyn and Bacon, 2001.

Fukundar-Parr, S. "What does feminization of poverty mean? It isn't just lack of income." *Feminist Economics* 5, no. 2 (1999): 99–103.

Gallegos, J. S., C. Tindall, & S. A. Gallegos. "The need for the advancement in conceptualization of cultural competence." *Advances in Social Work* 9, no. 1 (2008): 51–62.

Gandara, P. *California: A Case Study in the Loss of Affirmative Action*. The Civil Rights Project/Proyoecto Derechos Civiles. Los Angeles: The University of California, 2012.

Garces, L. M. *The Impact of Affirmative Action Bans in Graduate Education*. The Civil Rights Project/Proyoecto Derechos Civiles. Los Angeles: The University of California, 2012.

Garces, L. M., & D. Mickey-Pabello. "Racial diversity in the medical profession: The impact of affirmative action bans on underrepresented student of color matriculation in medical schools." *The Journal of Higher Education* 86, no. 2 (2015): 254–294.

Gratz v. Bolinger, 123 S.Ct.2323, 2339 (2003). https://www.wcl.american.edu/journal/genderlaw/11/fata.pdf.

Guidance on Constitutionally Protected Prayer in Public Elementary and Secondary Schools. US Department of Education, February 7, 2003. http://www.ed.gov/policy/gen/guid/religionandschools/prayer_guidance.html.

Hamm, B. "Democracy in the light of globalization." In M. Mannermaa, J. Dator, & P. Tiihonen (eds.), *Democracy and Futures*, 100–112. Helsinki, Finland: The Committee for the Future, 2006.

Hardtke, Erin M. "Elimination of race as a factor in school admissions: An analysis of *Hopwood v. Texas*." *Marquette Law Review* 80, no. 4 (1997): 1135–1146.

Harvard Civil Rights Project. "Constitutional requirements for affirmative action in higher education admissions and financial aid." Paper from Research Roundtable: Affirmative Action in Higher Education and K–12, Cambridge, MA, 2001.

Hassan, S. M., & K. Ahmad. "Globalization: Feminization of poverty and need for gender responsive social protection in Pakistan." *Pakistan Vision* 15, no. 2 (2014): 58–80.

Hegewisch, Ariane, Emily Ellis, & Heidi Hartmann. "The gender wage gap: 2014; Earning differences by race and ethnicity." Institute for Women's Policy Research, March 6, 2015. https://iwpr.org/publications/the-gender-wage-gap-2014-earnings-differences-by-race-and-ethnicity/.

Hegewisch, Ariane, & Williams-Baron, Emily. "The gender wage gap by occupation 2017 and by race and ethnicity." Institute for Women's Policy Research, April 9, 2018. https://iwpr.org/publications/gender-wage-gap-occupation-2017-race-ethnicity/.

Heller, Kristen. "Helm's white racial identity model." Last modified November 23, 2014. https://prezi.com/owhxtvs2yeed/helms-white-racial-identity-model/.

Herz, B. K., & G. B. Sperling. *What Works in Girls' Education: Evidence and Policies from the Developing World*. New York: Council on Foreign Relations, 2004.

"History of Proposition 187." California Coalition for Immigration Reform. http://ccir.nt/REFERENCE/187-History.html.

Hossain, K. I. "Understanding Islam in the U.S. classroom: A guide for elementary school teachers." *Multicultural Education* 20, no. 2 (2013): 49–52.

Hossain, K. I. "White privilege: Perceptions of pre-service teachers." *Multicultural Education* 23, no. 1 (2015): 52–55.

Hossenini, Khalid. *A Thousand Splendid Suns*. New York: Riverhead Books, 2007.

Hunt v. McNair, 413 U.S. 734 (1973). Findlaw.com. http://caselaw.lp.findlaw.com/scripts/getcase.pl?court=us&vol=413&invol=734.

Ifedili, A. J., & C. A. Ifedili. "An evaluation of Beijing 1995 on the appointments and promotions of Nigerian women to decision-making positions." *Education* 130, no. 1 (2009): 118–128.

Ijaz, Aisha, & Tahir Abbas. "The impact of inter-generational change on the attitudes of working-class South Asian Muslim parents on the education of their daughters." *Gender and Education* 22, no. 3 (2010): 313–326.

Illinois Department of Public Health. "Facts about violence against women." http://www.idph.state.il.us/about/womenshealth/factsheets/viol.htm.

International Organization for Migration. "Global migration trends factsheet, 2015." http://gmdac.iom.int/global-migration-trends-factsheet.

Jankowski, P.J., S. J. Sandage, & P. C. Hill. "Differentiations-based models of forgiveness, mental health and social justice commitment: Mediator effects for differentiation of self and humility." *Journal of Positive Psychology* 8, no. 5 (2013): 412–424.

Jochim, A., & P. McGuinn. "The politics of the Common Core Assessments." *Education Next* 16, no. 4 (2016): 44–52.

John Doe, Individually; Mary Doe, Individually and as Natural mother of A. Roe, B. Roe, and C. Roe, . . . v. Sue Porter, Individually and as Superintendent of the Rhea County School System . . . , United States Court of Appeals for the Sixth Circuit, 2004. Findlaw.com. https://caselaw.findlaw.com/us-6th-circuit/1054454.html.

Jokinen-Gordon, H. "Still penalized? Parity, age at first birth, and women's income in later life." *Journal of Women & Aging* 24, no. 3 (2012): 227–241.

Jones, G. S. "An end to poverty: The French Revolution and the promise of a world beyond want." Paper presented at the Anglo-American Conference of Historians at the University of London, July 7–9, 2004.

Kearns, L. "The construction of 'illiterate' and 'literate' youth: The effects of high-stakes standardized literacy testing." *Race, Ethnicity and Education* 19, no. 1 (2016): 121–140.

Kearns, L. "High stakes standardized testing and marginalized youth: An examination of the impact on those who fail." *Canadian Journal of Education* 34, no. 2 (2011): 112–130

Killenbeck, M. R. *Affirmative Action and Diversity: The Beginning of the End? Or the End of the Beginning?* Princeton, NJ: Policy Information Center, 2004.

Kime, P. "Incidents of rape in military much higher than previously reported." *Military Times*, December 4, 2014. https://www.militarytimes.com/2014/12/04/incidents-of-rape-in-military-much-higher-than-previously-reported/.

Kinkade, L. "America's poor becoming more destitute under Trump, UN report says." CNN.com, June 6, 2018. Accessed 6/23/2018. https://www.cnn.com/2018/06/22/us/america-poverty-un-report/index.html.

Komlosy, A., M. Boatca, & H. Nolte. "Introduction: Coloniality of power and hegemonic shifts in the world-system." *Journal of World-Systems Research, 22*, no. 2 (2016): 309–314.

Landsberg, B. K. "Affirmative action: What is the law?" Paper presented at the California School Boards Association, Long Beach, CA, November 30 to December 3, 1995.

Lapchick, R., J. Fox, A. Guiao, & M. Simpson. *The 2014 Racial and Gender Report Card: College Sport.* Orlando: The Institute for Diversity and Ethics in Sport, 2015.

Lapchick, R., A. Fuller, A. Boyd, B. Estrella, C. Lee, & N. Bredikhina. *The 2017 Racial and Gender Report Card: College Sport*. Orlando: University of Central Florida, 2018.

Latif, A. "A critical analysis of school enrollment and literacy rates of girls and women in Pakistan." *Educational Studies* 45, no. 5 (2009): 424–439.

Leach, M. M., J. T. Behrens, & N. K. La Fleur. "White racial identity and white racial consciousness: Similarities, differences, and recommendations." *Journal of Multicultural Counseling and Development* 30, no. 2 (2002): 66–80.

League of Women Voters. "History." https://www.lwv.org/about-us/history.

Lee, Amanda. "U.S. poverty thresholds and poverty guidelines: What's the difference?" PRB.org, 2018. https://www.prb.org/insight/u-s-poverty-thresholds-and-poverty-guidelines-whats-the-difference/.

Lee, E. "Revisioning cultural competencies in clinical social work practice." *Families in Society* 91, no. 3 (2010): 272–279.

Leibowitz, A. H. "English literacy: Legal sanction for discrimination." *Notre Dame Lawyer* 45, no. 7 (1969): 7–67.

Leonardo, Zeus. "The color of supremacy: Beyond the discourse of 'white privilege.'" *Educational Philosophy and Theory* 36, no. 2 (2004): 137–152.

Levitt v. Committee for Public Education, U.S. Supreme Court, 413 U.S. 472, 1973. Findlaw.com. http://caselaw.lp.findlaw.com/scripts/getcase.pl?court=us&vol=413&invol=472.

Lieber, R. J., & R. E. Weisberg. "Globalization, culture, and identities in crisis." *International Journal of Politics, Culture and Society* 16, no. 2 (2002): 273–296.

Lin, C., & M. Lee. "A comparative policy analysis of family preservation programs in the U.S. and in Taiwan." *Journal of Child and Family Studies* 25, no. 4 (2015): 1131–1144.

Lum, D. *Cultural Competence, Practice Stages, and Client Systems: A Case Study Approach.* Belmont, CA: Thomson Brooks/Cole, 2004.

Maxwell, K. J. "League of Women Voters through the Decades!" League of Women Voters of the United States, 2007. http://lwv.org/contents/league-women-voters-through-decades.

Mazrui, A. A. *Cultural Forces in World Politics.* Nairobi: Heinemann, 1990.

Mba, N. E. *Nigerian Women Mobilized: Women's Political Activity in Southern Nigeria 1900–1965.* Berkeley: University of California Press, 1982.

McCarthy, Justin. "Americans' assessments of living standards brighter in 2015 (January 6, 2016)." Gallup.com, 2016. https://news.gallup.com/poll/188048/americans-assessments-living-standards-brighter015.aspx?g_source=link_NEWSV9&g_medium=TOPIC&g_campaign=item_&g_content=Americans%27%2520Assessments%2520of%2520Living%2520Standards%2520Brighter%2520in%25202015.

McCollum v. Board of Education, 333 U.S. 203 (1948). Justia.com. https://supreme.justia.com/cases/federal/us/333/203/case.html.

McFarland, Susan. "U.N. report: With 40M in poverty, U.S. most unequal developed nation." UPI.com, 2018. https://www.upi.com/UN-report-With-40M-in-poverty-US-most-unequal-developed-nation/8671529664548/.

McIntosh, P. "White privilege: Unpacking the invisible knapsack." *Peace and Freedom* 49, no. 4 (1989): 10–12.

The Medicaid and CHIP Payment and Access Commission. "History and impact of CHIP." https://www.macpac.gov/subtopic/history-and-impact-of-chip/.

Megahed, N., & S. Lack. "Colonial legacy, women's rights and gender-educational inequality in the Arab world with particular reference to Egypt and Tunisia." *International Review of Education* 57, no. 3/4 (2011): 397–418.

Mohamed, B. "New estimates show U.S. Muslim population continues to grow." Washington, DC: Pew Research Center, 2018. http://www.pewresearch.org/fact-tank/2018/01/03/new-estimates-show-u-s-muslim-population-continues-to-grow/.

Mohammadpur, A., J. Karimi, & M. Alizadeh. "Women and culture of poverty (a qualitative study of the culture of poverty among the Iranian caretaker women)." *Quality and Quantity* 48, no. 1 (2014): 1–14.

Montz, J. K., & A. Zajacova. "Why is life expectancy declining among low-educated women in the United States?" *American Journal of Public Health* 104, no. 10 (2014): e5–e7.

Moses, Michele S., Amy Farley, Matthew Gaertner, Christina H. Paguyo, Darrell D. Jackson, & Kenneth R. Rowe. *Investigating the Defeat of Colorado's Amendment 46: An Analysis of the Trends and Principal Factors Influencing Voter Behaviors.* Boulder, CO: University of Colorado, 2010.

Moses, M. S., J. T. Yun, & P. Marin. "Affirmative Action's fate: Are 20 years more years enough?" *Education Policy Analysis Archives* 17, no. 17 (2009): 1–38.

"Most of California's Prop. 187 ruled unconstitutional." CNN.com, 1998. http://www.cnn.com/ALLPOLITICS/1998/03/19/propo.187.

MPH@GW. "Poverty vs. federal poverty level." https://publichealthonline.gwu.edu/blog/poverty-vs-federal-poverty-level/.

The Nation. "151 years of America's housing history." TheNation.com, 2018. https://www.thenation.com/article/americas-housing-history/.

National Association of Working Women, "About 9to5." 9to5.org, n.d. https://9to5.org/about-9to5/.

National Center for Education Statistics. *Digest of Education Statistics: 2005.* Washington, DC: U.S. Department of Education, Institute of Education Sciences, 2006.

National Coalition for Women and Girls in Education (NCWGE). *Title IX at 35.* Washington, DC: National Coalition for Women and Girls in Education, 2008.

National Coalition for Women and Girls in Education (NCWGE). *Title IX at 30: Report Card on Gender Equity.* Washington, DC: National Coalition for Women and Girls in Education, 2002.

National Council of Negro Women, Inc. "Our Mission." NCNW.org, 2018. http://ncnw.org/ncnw/our-mission.

National Population Commission. *Nigeria Demographic and Education Survey, Adapted from Nigeria Demographic and Health Survey 2003.* Abuja, Nigeria: National Population Commission, 2004.

National Science Foundation. *Women, Minorities, and Persons with Disabilities in Science and Engineering: 2004.* Arlington, VA: National Science Foundation, Division of Science Resources Statistics, 2004.

NCPP. *Child Poverty*, 2018. http://www.nccp.org/topics/childpoverty.html.

NCPP. *Children's Mental Health*, 2018. http://www.nccp.org/topics/mentalhealth.html.

New Media Consortium. *Horizon Report: Higher Education Edition.* Austin, TX: New Media Consortium, 2017.

Niyozov, S. "Teachers and teaching Islam and Muslims in pluralistic societies: Claims, misunderstandings, and responses." *Journal of International Migration & Integration* 11, no. 1 (2010): 23–40.

No Child Left Behind. http://www.ed.gov/nclb/overview/intro/presidentplan.

NURU International. "Extreme poverty," n.d. http://www.nuruinternational.org/why/extreme-poverty/.

Obergefell, James et al., petitioners, v. Richard Hodges, director, Ohio Department of Health, et al. 135 S. Ct. 1732 (2015). https://scholar.google.com/scholar_case?case=7448548918964847101&q=Obergefel+v.+Hodges&hl=en&as_sdt=2006&as_vis=1.

Oliver, M. "The social construction of racial privilege in the United States: An asset perspective." In C. V. Hamilton, L. Huntley, N. Alexander, A. S. A. Guiaraes, & W. James (eds.), *Beyond Racism*, 251–272. London: Lynne Rienner Publishers, 2001.

Olverio, A., & Lauderdale. "The world system according to Andre Gunder Frank: Hegemony and domination." *Journal of World-Systems Research* 21, no. 1 (2016): 184–192.

Onsongo, J. "Affirmative action, gender equity and university admission—Kenya, Uganda, and Tanzania." *London Review of Education* 7, no. 1 (2009): 71–81.

Oxford Poverty and Human Development Initiative (OPHI). "Policy—A multidimensional approach." https://ophi.org.uk/policy/multidimensional-poverty-index/.

Oplatka, I., & O. Lapidot. "Muslim women in graduate studies: Some insights into the accessibility of higher education for minority women students." *Studies in Higher Education* 37 no. 3 (2012): 327–344.

Ortega, R. M., & K. C. Faller. "Training child welfare workers from an intersectional cultural perspective: A paradigm shift." *Child Welfare* 90, no. 5 (2011): 27–49.

Paddock, Adam. "The women's war of 1929." Accessed 09/25/18. http://oxfordre.com/africanhistory/view/10.1093/acrefore/9780190277734.001.0001/acrefore-9780190277734-e-271?rskey=c60HPs&result=1.

Paine, David R., Peter J. Jankowski, & Steven J. Sandage. "Humility as a predictor of intercultural competence: Mediator effects for differentiation-of-self." *The Family Counseling Journal: Counseling and Therapy for Couples and Families* 24, no. 1 (2016): 15–22.

Partnership for 21st Century Learning. "Framework for 21st Century Learning." Battelleforkids.org, 2007. http://www.battelleforkids.org/networks/p21/frameworks-resources.

Pearce, D. "The feminization of poverty: Women, work, and welfare." *The Urban & Social Change Review* 11, no. 1/2 (1978): 28–36

Pense, S. L., B. W. Freeburg, & C. A. Clemons, "Implementation of Common Core State Standards: Choices, positions, and frames." *Career and Technical Education Research* 40, no. 3 (2015): 157–173.

Peterson, P. E., M. B. Henderson, M. R. West, & S. Barrows, "Common Core brand taints opinion on standards: 2016 findings and 10-year trends from the EdNext Poll." *Education Next* 17, no. 1 (2017): 8–28.

Pew Research Center. "Origins and destinations of the world's migrants, from 1990–2017." Pewglobal.org, February 28, 2018. http://www.pewglobal.org/2018/02/28/global-migrant-stocks/?country=US&date=2017.

Pew Research Center. "America's changing religious landscape." Pew Research Center, Demographic Study, May 12, 2015. http://www.pewforum.org/2015/05/12/americas-changing-religious-landscape/.

Pew Research Center. "U.S. public becoming less religious." pewforum.org, Polling and Analysis, November 3, 2015. www.pewforum.org/2015/11/03/u-s-public-becoming-less-religious/.

Phinney, J. S. "Ethnic identity in adolescents and adults." *Review of the Research Psychological Bulletin* 108, no. 3 (1990): 499–514.

Pigozzi, M. J. "A UNESCO view of global citizenship education." *Educational Review 58* no. 1 (2006): 1–4.

Plessy v. Ferguson, 163.u.s.537 [1896].

Plummer, R. "Black Brazil seeks a better future." *BBC News*, September 25, 2006. http://newsvote.bbc.co.uk/mpapps/pagetools/print/news.bbc.co.uk/2/hi/americas/5357842.stm.

Quigley, C. N. *Constitutional Democracy.* Calabasas, CA: Center for Civic Education, n.d.

Race: The Power of an Illusion. PBS, 2003. A three-part documentary produced by California Newsreel; directed by Christine Herbes-Sommers, Tracy Heather Strain, & Llewellyn Smith.

Rape, Abuse & Incest National Network, "Victims of sexual violence: Statistics." https://www.rainn.org/statistics/victims-sexual-violence.

Reynolds v. United States. 98 U.S. 145. (1878). http://www.law.umkc.edu/faculty/projects/ftrials/conlaw/reynoldsvus.html.

"*Reynolds v. United States*." Berkeley Center for Religion, Peace, and World Affairs. https://berkleycenter.georgetown.edu/cases/reynolds-v-united-states.

"*Reynolds v. United States*." Oyez.org. https://www.oyez.org/cases/1850-1900/98us145.

Riley, C. "Religious expression in public schools." Archived information, United States Department of Education. *The Secretary*, 1998. http://www.ed.gov/policy/gen/guid/religionandschools/prayer_guidance.html.

Robinson, W. "Introduction: Globalization and race in world capitalism." *Journal of World-Systems Research* 22, no. 1 (2016): 3–8.

Roche, Kristen. "Millennials and the gender wage gap in the U.S.: A cross-cohort comparison of young workers born in the 1960s and the 1980s." *Atlantic Economic Journal* 45, no. 3 (2017): 333–350.

Roser, M., & E. Ortiz-Ospina. "Global extreme poverty." OurWorldInData.org, 2013. https://ourworldindata.org/extreme-poverty.

Rowe, W., S. K. Bennett, & D. R. Atkinson. "White racial identity models: A critique and alternative proposal. *Counseling Psychologist* 22, no. 1 (1994): 129–146.

Rubery, J., & A. Rafferty. "Women and recession revisited." *Work, Employment and Society* 27, no. 3 (2013): 414–432. doi:10.1177/0950017012460314.

Running, K., & L. M. Roth. "To wed or work? Assessing work and marriage as routes out of poverty." *Journal of Poverty* 17, no. 2 (2013): 177–197.

Ryan, C. L., & K. Bauman. "Educational attainment in the United States: 2015." https://www.census.gov/content/dam/Census/library/publications/2016/demo/p20-578.pdf.

Schenker, Jennifer L. "The networked economy: How technology, innovation, and venture capital are transforming the future of mobile." *Informilo*, February 25–28, 2013. https://www.ifc.org/wps/wcm/connect/1e6610804ef016539b82db3eac88a2f8/Mobilizing-Women.pdf?MOD=AJPERES.

School District of Abington Township, Pennsylvania et al. v. Schempp et al. 374 U.S. 203(1963). http://www.nationalcenter.org/scot63.htm.

"*School District of Abington Township, Pennsylvania v. Schempp.*" Oyez.org. https://www.oyez.org/cases/1962/142.

Schugurensky, D. "Elementary and secondary school act, the 'war on poverty' and title 1." In D. Schugurensky (ed.), *History of education: Selected moments of the 20th century*, 1996–2011. http://schugurensky.faculty.asu.edu/moments/index.html.

Schultz, L. J., & J. C. Fortune. *The Three I's: Sources of Test Bias*. Washington, DC: Virginia Polytechnic Institute, 2001.

Seubert, S. "Dynamics of modern citizenship democracy and peopleness in a global era." *Constellations* 21, no. 4 (2014): 547–559.

Shannon, J. "Reading results: A critical look at standardized testing and the linguistic minority." Master of Science in Education degree thesis submitted to School of Education, Dominican University of California, 2008.

Shannon, T. R. *An Introduction to the World-System Perspective*. New York: Westview Press, 1992.

Shauman, Kimberlee A. "Gender differences in the early employment outcomes of STEM doctorates." *Social Sciences* 6, no. 1 (2017): 24.

Sheykhjan, T. M., K. Rajeswari, & K. Jabari, "Empowerment of women through education in the twenty-first century." Proceedings of the National Education Meet: Mapping New Terrains for 21st Century Women, Nalanchira, Thiruvanthapram, Kerala, India, 2014.

Shillington, Kevin. *History of Africa*. London: Palgrave Macmillan, 2012.

Slaughter, J. B. *After Michigan, What? Next Steps for Affirmative Action.* Education Policy Institute, Policy Perspectives. www.educationalpolicy.org.

Snider, J. S., S. Reysen, & I. Katzarska-Miller. "How we frame the message of globalization matters." *Journal of Applied Social Psychology* 43, no. 8 (2013): 1599–1607.

Sony, K. C., Bishnu Raj Upreti, & Bashu Prasad Subedi. "'We know the taste of sugar because of cardamom production': Links among commercial cardamom farming, women's involvement in production, and the feminization of poverty." *Journal of International Women's Studies* 18, no. 1 (2016): 181–207.

Springer, A. *Update on Affirmative Action in Higher Education: A Current Legal Overview*. Washington, DC: American Association of University Professors, 2003.

Steele, C. M. "A threat in the air: How stereotypes shape intellectual identity and performance." *American Psychologist* 52, no. 6 (1997): 613–629.

Stone v. Graham, 449 U.S. 39, 1980. Findlaw.com. http://caselaw.lp.findlaw.com/scripts/getcase.pl?court=us&vol=449&invol=39.

Stowasser, B. F. *Women in the Qur'an, Traditions and Interpretations*. New York: Oxford University Press, 1994.

Stride, G. T., & Caroline Ifeka. *People and Empires of West Africa: West Africa in History 1000–1800*. Edinburgh: Thomas Nelson and Sons, Ltd., 1971.

Supreme Court of the United States Syllabus: *Lee et al. v. Weisman*, Personally and as next Friend of Weisman: Certiorari to the United States Court of Appeals for the First Circuit. (1992). http://supct.law.cornell.edu/supc/html/90-1014.ZS.html.

Swartz, Sharlene, Emma Arogundade, & Danya Davis. "Unpacking (white) privilege in a South African university classroom: A neglected element in multicultural educational contexts." *Journal of Moral Education* 43, no. 3 (2014): 345–361.

Sylvers, Eric. "Mobilizing women: The industry is now focusing on closing the mobile gender gap." *Informilo*, February 25–28, 2013. https://www.ifc.org/wps/wcm/connect/1e6610804ef016539b82db3eac88a2f8/Mobilizing-Women.pdf?MOD=AJPERES

Tandon, Yash. "What is global apartheid and why do we fight it?" *Pambazuka News*, March 18, 2010. https://www.pambazuka.org/global-south/what-global-apartheid-and-why-do-we-fight-it.

Taylor, John E. "30 years after *Edwards v. Aguillard*: Why creationism lingers in public schools." *Conversation*, 2018. http://theconversation.com/30-years-after-edwards-v-aguillard-why-creationism-lingers-in-public-schools-79603.

Terrie, C. *Giving a Little Help to Girls? Evidence on Grade Discrimination and Its Effect on Students' Achievement.* London: Center for Economic Performance, 2005.

Tervalon, M., & J. Murray-Garcia. "Cultural humility versus cultural competence: A critical distinction in defining physician training outcomes in multicultural education." *Journal of Health Care for the Poor and Underserved* 9 (1998): 117–125.

Thibos, M., D. Lavin-Loucks, & M. Martin. "The feminization of poverty." A report prepared for the 2007 Joint Policy Forum on the Feminization of Poverty, sponsored by The William Institute and the YWCA, May 7, 2007.

U.S. Department of Justice. *Title VI of the Civil Rights Act of 1964* 42 U.S.C. https://www.justice.gov/crt/fcs/TitleVI-Overview.

Tjaden, P., & N. Thoennes. *Full Report of the Prevalence, Incidence, and Consequences of Violence against Women* Washington, DC: National Institute of Justice, Office of Justice Programs, U.S. Department of Justice, and the Centers for Disease Control and Prevention, 2000.

Trygged, S., E. Hedlund, & I. Kareholt. "Beaten and poor? A study of the long-term economic situation of women victims of severe violence." *Social Work in Public Health* 29, no. 2 (2014): 100–113.

UNICEF. "Children bear the brunt of poverty." UNICEF.org, 2017. http://data.unicef.org/topic/overview/child-poverty/#.

UNICEF. "Ending extreme poverty: A focus on children." UNICEF.org, 2016. http://data.unicef.org/wp-content/uploads/2017/09/Ending_Extreme_Poverty_A_Focus_on_Children_Oct_2016.pdf.

United Nations. *Shame of War: Sexual Violence against Women and Girls in Conflict.* Nairobi: United Nations Office for the Coordination of Humanitarian Affairs Integrated Regional Information Network, 2007.

United Nations. *Beijing Declaration and Platform for Action.* New York: United Nations, 1995.

United Nations. "World Summit for Social Development." UN.org, 1995. https://www.un.org/development/desa/dspd/world-summit-for-social-development-1995.html.

United Nations. *Declaration on the Elimination of Violence against Women*, Article 1. 1993. http://www.un.org/documents/ga/res/48/a48r104.htm.

United Nations. *Convention on the Elimination of All Forms of Discrimination Against Women*, Article 1. 1979. Resolution Adopted by the United Nations General Assembly 2263 (XXII), Twenty-Second Session, New York.

United Nations. *Resolution Adopted by the General Assembly 3520 (XXX).* 1975. World Conference of the International Women's Year. Thirtieth Session, Agenda Item 75, New York.

United Nations. *Convention on Consent to Marriage, Minimum Age for Marriage and Registration of Marriage.* 1962. Resolution Adopted by the General Assembly of the United Nations 1763 A (XVII) November 7.

United Nations. *Convention on the Nationality of Married Women*, Chapter XVI. 1957. Status of Women. New York.

United Nations. Convention on the Political Rights of Women, Chapter XVI. 1953. Status of Women. New York.

United Nations, Division for Sustainable Development. "Sustainable Development Goal 1: End poverty in all its forms everywhere." 2017. https://sustainabledevelopment.un.org/sdg1.

United Nations, Division for Sustainable Development. "Transforming our world: The 2030 Agenda for Sustainable Development." 2015. https://sustainabledevelopment.un.org/post2015/transformingourworld.

United Nations Population Fund. "Migration." http://www.unfpa.org/migration.

United States Department of Education. "Report to the White House Council on Women and Girls." U.S. Department of Education Agency Report, July 6, 2010.

United States Department of Justice. "Overview of Title IX of the Education Amendment of 1972, U.S.C. A§ 1681 ET. SEQ." https://www.justice.gov/crt/overview-title-ix-education-amendments-1972-20-usc-1681-et-seq.

United States Department of Labor. *Title IX, Education Amendment of 1972.* https://www.dol.gov/oasam/regs/statutes/titleix.htm.

United States Department of Labor. "Latest Annual Data." United States Department of Labor, Women's Bureau. http://www.dol.gov/wb/stats/stats_data.htm.

United States General Accounting Office. *Women's Educational Equity Act. A Review of Program Goals and Strategies Needed.* Report to Congressional Requesters, December, 1994.

United States Housing Act of 1937. http://www.bostonfairhousing.org/timeline/.

University of California Regents v. Bakke (1978), No. 76-811. Findlaw.com. http://caselaw.findlaw.com/us-supreme-court/438/265.html.

U.S. Equal Employment Opportunities Commission. *Title VII of the Civil Rights Act of 1964.* https://www.eeoc.gov/laws/statutes/titlevii.cfm.

U.S. Department of Education. "Attachment A: Summary of principal flexibility provisions in the Elementary and Secondary Education Act (ESEA)." http://www2.ed.gov/nclb/freedom/local/flexibility/summary.pdf.

U.S. Department of Education. *Digest of Education Statistics: 2005.* Washington DC: Institute of Education Sciences, 2005.

U.S. Department of Education. *Every Student Succeeds Act (ESSA).* http://www.ed.gov/essa?src=rn.

U.S. Department of Education. *Improving Basic Programs Operated by Local Educational Agencies (Title 1, Part A).* https://www.sdcoe.net/student-services/student-support/Pages/improving-basic-programs.aspx.

U.S. Department of Education. Laws & Guidance: Elementary and Secondary Education. http://www.ed.gov/policy/elsec/leg/esea02.

U.S. Department of Education. *Title I — Improving the academic achievement of the disadvantaged.* http://www2.ed.gov/policy/elsec/leg/esea02/pg1.html.

U.S. Department of Education. "Results in Brief: Early Implementation of State Differentiated Accountability Plans under the No Child Left Behind Act." 2012. Retrieved from http://www2.ed.gov/about/offices/list/opepd/ppss/reports.html.

U.S. Department of Education. "Results in Brief: Implementing Accountability and Supports under ESEA flexibility." http://www2.ed.gov/about/offices/list/opepd/ppss/reports.html.

U. S. Department of Education. *Title I – Improving the Academic Achievement of the Disadvantaged.* http://www.ed.gov/policy/elsec/leg/esea02.

U.S. Department of Education (USDE). *National Excellence: A Case for Developing America's Talent.* Washington D.C. USDE, 1993.

U.S. Department of Health and Human Services. *Cultural Competence Works: Using Cultural Competence to Improve the Quality of Health Care for Diverse Populations and Add Value to Managed Care Arrangement.* Merrifield, VA: Health Resources and Administration, 2001.

U.S. Department of Housing and Urban Development (HUD). "US Housing Act of 1947, as amended." https://www.hud.gov/sites/documents/DOC_10010.pdf.

U.S. Department of Housing and Urban Development (HUD). *Programs of HUD.* Washington, DC: U.S. Department of Housing and Urban Development, 2017.

U.S. Equal Employment Opportunities Commission. *Title VII of the Civil Rights Act of 1964.* https://www.eeoc.gov/laws/statutes/titlevii.cfm.

Utah State University. *Students with Attention Deficit Disorders ADD/ADHD: Eligibility Issues and Service Options under the Individuals with Disabilities Education Act (IDEA) and Section 504.* Logan, UT: Utah State University, 1998.

Valentin, I. *Title IX: A Brief History; 25 Years of Title IX. WEEA Digest.* Newton, MA: WEEA Equity Resource Center at EDC, 1997.

Wale, Kim, & Don Foster. "Investing in discourse of poverty and development: How white wealthy South Africans mobilize meaning to maintain privilege." *South African Review of Sociology* 38, no. 1 (2007): 45–69.

Ward, J., C. Turner, J. Watts, & J. Eldred. "Every woman's right to learn." *Adult Learning* 22, no. 6 (2011): 12–13.

Warner, J. *The Women's Leadership Gap.* Washington DC: Center for American Progress, 2014.

Williams, G. W. *History of the Negro Race in America from 1619–1880: Negroes as Slaves, as Soldiers, and as Citizens* (2 vols.). New York: G.P. Putnam's Sons, 1885.

Wootton, B. H. "Gender differences in occupational employment." *Monthly Labor Review* 120, no. 4 (April 1997): 15–24.

World Economic Forum. *The Global Gender Gap Report 2013.* Geneva, Switzerland: World Economic Forum, 2013.

World Health Organization. "Global Health Observatory (GHO) data." https://www.who.int/gho/en/.

World Health Organization. "Violence against women: Intimate partner and sexual violence against women." WHO, November 29, 2017. http://www.who.int/mediacentre/factsheets/fs239/en/.

Wooden v. NAACP. Findlaw.com. https://caselaw.findlaw.com/us-11thcircuit/1140908.html.

World Health Organization, *Millennium Development Goals (MDGs)*, 2018. http://www.who.int/topics/millennium_development_goals/about/en/.

Zhao, Y. "A world at risk: An imperative for a paradigm shift to cultivate 21st century learners." *Society* 52, no. 2 (April 2015): 129–135.

Zhao, Z. "Empowerment in a socialist egalitarian agenda: Minority women in China's higher education system." *Gender and Education* 23, no. 4 (2011): 431–445.

Zhibin, L. "Chinese women and poverty alleviation: Reflections and prospects for the future." *Chinese Sociology and Anthropology* 40, no. 4 (2008): 27–37.

Zorach v. Clauson, 1952. Findlaw.com. https://caselaw.findlaw.com/us-supreme-court/343/306.html.

Zukas, L. L. "Women's war of 1929." Revolution Protest Encyclopedia. http://www.revolutionprotestencyclopedia.com/fragr_image/media/IEOWomens_War_of_1929.

Zurcher, A. J. "Citizenship." In Lauren S. Bahr & Bernard Johnston (eds.), *Collier's Encyclopedia*, 447. New York: Macmillan Educational Company, 1992.

Index

Aba Women's Riot, 55, 56–58
Abington School District v. Schempp, 89
aboriginal, 42
Affirmative Action, 33–46 *passim*
Africa, 2–4, 7, 9–10, 15–16, 23–24, 42, 49
African
   American, 10, 34, 43–45, 47, 107, 109, 111–112
   countries, 42, 48
   governments, 7, 42, 51–52, 56, 61
   peoples, 3, 61
   slaves, 3, 9, 42, 87, 95, 108
   studies, 27, 47
   traditional societies, 3, 51, 53, 56
Alabama A&M University, 41
Alabama State University, 35, 41
American
   children, 60, 106–107, 114
   colonies, 2, 5, 100
   culture, 5–6
   education, 10, 85, 43–45, 95–96
   educational context, 10, 15, 24
   educational system, 27–30, 87
   families, 46
   frontier, 86
   government, 44, 90, 106

   history, 10, 33, 71, 86, 95, 107–111
   idea, 41
   journalist, 9
   life, 75
   middle class, 34, 108
   people, 16
   public schools, 33, 81, 85–102 *passim*
   religious landscape, 87
   society, 5–6, 34
   students, 28, 30–31, 41, 96
   women, 58–60, 69, 72, 77, 81, 83
Appalachian region, 46, 108
apartheid, 4
   gender, and, 79
   global, 15
   South Africa, and, 7
Arab nations, 23, 48, 55, 61

Banks, James, vii
Benin, 3
Bethune, Mary McLeod, 72
bigotry, 2
Boko Haram, 69
boundary(ies)
   cultural, religious, social, 5, 27
   racial, 5–6
   national, 20, 22, 25, 35

Britain, 21, 49, 51, 60, 83, 100, 105
Brown v. Board of Education, 33–34
Bureau of Labor Statistics, 80, 82

Calabar, 56, 57
California, 37, 44, 74–75
capitalist, 9
  capitalist system, 16
Children's Health Insurance Program (CHIP), 104, 106, 114
Christianity
  schools, and, 10, 96
  United States, and, 86–88, 96
  Western mission, and, 9
Christianization, 9–10
citizenship
  cosmopolitan, 25
  global, 20, 21, 24–27
  minorities, and, 73
  United States, and, 111–112
  women, and, 63, 73
Civil Rights Act, 34–36, 39, 74–77 *passim*
Clinton, Bill, 44, 90, 93–94, 111, 114
Clinton, Hillary, 72, 114
colonial, 1–17 *passim*, 48, 50–51, 55–57
colonization, 3, 10
Colorado, 45, 122n31
Common Core State Standards, 28, 30–32
communication, 13, 16, 20, 22–24, 29–29, 34, 48
  modalities, 13
  technology, and, 34
communist, 48
community
  Christian, 96
  European, 60
  global, 1–17 *passim*, 21–22
  political, 24
competence, 12
competency
  cross-cultural, 27–28
  cultural, 11–13, 27
  intercultural, 11

consciousness, 37
  racial, 5–6
Constitution of the United States, 72, 86, 88–90, 100–101
  constitutional, 34–36, 43–44, 46, 78, 86, 94–95, 101–102
Convention on the Elimination of All Forms of Discrimination against Women, 65–66
cooperation, 3, 110
Court of Appeals, 38–39
creationism, 92, 101–102
cross-cultural
  affirmations, 5
  competency, 27–28
  education, 24
  interactions, 11, 27–28
  relationships, 6
cultural, 53, 55, 59, 65
  humility, and, 2, 11–13
culture, 11, 20, 26–29
curriculum, 28–30
  educational, 24, 27–28, 55
  local, 28
  religion, and, 91–94, 102

Decade for Women, 65
democracy, 25
  crisis, and, 16
  United States, and, 44, 86
Department of Justice, 69
development, 29
  economic, 14–15, 65, 78
  curricula, and, 30
  identity, 5–6
  intercultural competency, and, 11–13
  gender, and, 50, 53–54, 64–65, 67–72 *passim*
  global citizenship, and, 25–26
  social, 110, 114
  technology, and, 24
Development Model of Intercultural Sensitivity (DMIS), 11–12

discrimination
  civil rights, and, 74–75
  educational, 33–38 *passim*, 40–46 *passim*
  gender, and, 50, 59, 62–63, 65–66, 73, 75–78
  racial, 11, 33–35, 37
  United States, and, 33–35
diversity, 25–26, 43
  cultural, 4, 11–12, 25
  educational, 35, 37, 43, 82–102 *passim*
  racial, 37
  religious, 85–102 *passim*
  United States, and, 10–11, 16, 20
divorce, 55–56, 58, 60–61
dominance
  European, 2–4, 15
  colonial legacy, and, 4
  religious, 86

economic
  development, 65
  equality, 66
  gender, and, 58, 60, 62, 75, 78
  history, and, 107–110
  inequality, 11, 14, 17, 107–110
  justice, 25–26, 77
  opportunities, 10, 24, 48
  privilege, 6–7
  resources, 15
Edwards v. Aguillard, 101–102
Efik people, 57
Egypt, 50–51, 54, 55–56
Emancipation Proclamation, 108
employment, 8, 33–35, 42, 44, 49, 53, 58–60, 73–76, 80–81, 108
enculturation, 6
Engel v. Vitale, 99–101
Equal Employment Opportunities Commission (EEOC), 73
Equal Pay Act, 73
Equal Protection Clause of the Fourteenth Amendment, 36, 38–40

equity
  gender, global, and, 42, 47–70 *passim*
  gender, United States, and, 71–84 *passim*
Establishment Clause of the First Amendment, 88–90, 100–102
ethnic minorities, 6, 10–11, 34, 43, 45–46, 114
ethnocentrism, 2, 12, 25
Europe, 3–4, 7, 14–17, 21, 32, 61, 87, 107
European, 3–5, 15–16
  worldviews, 3–4
European Union, 17, 21
evolution, 91–94, 101
exclusion, 6, 34, 48, 104

Family and Medical Leave Act, 77
female
  activists, 71–72
  earnings, and, 82–83
  education, and, 42, 54, 81
  industry, and, 82
  literacy, and, 50
  poverty, and, 58–62
  sexual assault, and, 69
First Amendment of the United States Constitution, 86, 88–90, 98–102
foreign, 3, 4, 17, 23
Free Exercise Clause of the First Amendment, 88–90

gender, 2, 14, 17, 28–29, 34, 42–44, 47–70 *passim*, 71–84 *passim*, 97, 110
Germany, 22–23, 83
globalization, 2, 10, 13, 15–16, 19–32 *passim*, 48
Gorbachev, Mikhail, 19, 21
Grand Rapids School District v. Ball, 102
Gratz v. Bollinger, et al., 35, 38–40
Greece, 22

hegemony, 15–16
hijab, 51, 55–56
Hispanics, 43, 45, 107–109
Hopwood v. University of Texas, 35, 38–40
human rights, 1, 25–27, 49, 53–54, 63–64, 65–67, 105, 110
humility, cultural, 2, 11–13

Igbo people, 3–4, 56–57
identity, 20, 28
   cultural, 20
   group, 43
   racial, 5–6
   self-, 25, 28
immigration, 20–22
instruction, 24, 27–30, 92, 94, 98–99, 101
   religious, 94, 98–99
intercultural, competency, 11, 13, 27
international
   immigration, 21–23
   knowledge, 24
   law, 1
   peace, 64
   trade, 32
International Year of Women, 64–65
Islam, 50, 51, 55–56
   education, and, 95–97
   Islamic, 49, 55

justice
   economic, 25, 77
   social, 50, 54, 67
Justice Powell, Lewis, 36–37, 40
jurisdiction, 34, 74

Kennedy, John F., 73
Kenya, 42
   Kenyan, 42
Kenya Certificate of Secondary Education (KCSE), 42

labor
   forced, 57

labor force, 54, 79, 80–82
leaders, 34
market, 83, 109
migrants, 23
organizations, 73–74
landscape(s),
   economic, 7
   educational, 24
   religious, 87
legacy
   admissions, 45–46
   colonial, 13
   historical, 5
Lemon v. Kurtzman, 101
Lily Ledbetter Fair Pay Act, 74, 77

marginalized, 7, 10, 48–49
market(s), 14, 16, 83, 108–109
marketplace, 16
marriage
   forced, 49, 53, 62
   United States, and, 60, 75
   women's rights, and, 55, 63–65
Marxist, 13–14
McCollum v. Board of Education, 98
Middle East, 23, 49, 58
migration, 16, 22–23, 61, 105
minority(ies), 11, 33–39, 41–42, 44–46, 86, 108, 112
   ethnic, 6, 10–11, 28, 43, 74, 86, 108, 112, 114
   gender, 28, 33–34, 74
   religious, 100
missionaries, 17
mobility, 16, 42, 107–108
modern, 14, 20, 55
modernization, 14
multicultural education, 2, 11, 27, 106, 115
multiculturalism, 5, 13, 19–32 *passim*
Muslim, 20, 22, 29, 49–53, 55–56, 58, 88, 93, 95–97

National Association of Working Women, 77

National Center for Children in Poverty (NCPP), 106–107
Negro, 34
New World Order, 19
Nigeria, 3, 16, 23, 28, 51–52, 55–58, 61, 69
Nineteenth Amendment to the US Constitution, 72
No Child Left Behind, 90

Obama, Barak, 19, 21, 31, 83, 114
opportunity(ies), 5–7, 10, 28–29, 33–46 *passim*, 48–49, 51, 53–54, 58, 61–62, 64, 71, 73–74, 76, 78, 103, 108–109
Owerri, 57
Oxford Poverty and Human Development Initiative (OPHI), 104–105

Pakistan, 49–50–53, 62
Partnership for 21st Century Learning, 29
periphery, 14–16
policy(ies)
　apartheid, and, 7
　discrimination, and, 1, 49, 59, 106, 108, 114
　civil rights, 40
　economic, 109, 111, 114
　educational, 34, 37, 42–43, 47
　social, 48, 110
　white privilege, and, 6
poor, 46, 58–62, 104–107, 109, 111–113, 115
Portugal, 2
postcolonial, 4, 14
poverty
　alleviation, 62, 111–112, 114–115
　child, 105–107
　elderly, 111
　female, 58–62
　multidimensional, 61, 104–105
Poverty Index, 104–106

power, 2–4, 11–12, 14–15, 56–57–74, 86, 115
prayer, in schools, 90, 92–94, 97, 99–102
Pregnancy Discrimination Act, 77
privilege, 2, 5–11, 45
Proposition 209 (California Affirmative Action), 44–45

Qatar, 23, 28
Qur'an, 55

race, 2, 4, 6–7, 9, 11, 14, 17, 29, 34–40, 44, 54, 64, 74, 76, 77–78, 82, 107
rape, 69
Regents of the University of California v. Bakke, 35–37, 43
religion, 5, 20, 53, 56, 64, 74, 76, 85–102 *passim*
respect, 1, 3, 7, 25–29, 64, 86
responsibility
　citizenship, and, 25–26
　cultural, 2, 5, 6–7
Reynolds vs. the United States, 86, 88
Roosevelt, Eleanor, 72
Roosevelt, Franklin Delano, 34

Saudi Arabia, 61
Separate but Equal, 34
social inclusion, 48
social isolation, 48
social justice, 54
society(ies)
　cultural norms, and, 50
　destabilized, 9
　education, and, 32, 51, 96
　globalization, and, 19–20, 22–24
　global, 21, 27, 29
　healthy, 2, 33, 48, 50, 54
　homogenous, 56
　institutional racism in, 7, 10, 35, 41
　modern, 13–14
　non-Western, 15
　traditional, 53

United States, and, 5–6, 10, 34, 35, 86, 96
  Western, 16, 49, 96
  women, and, 48–53 *passim*, 54–55, 64, 65, 71
socio-political, 16
South Africa, 3, 7, 10, 15
standard(s)
  admissions, 38, 41
  Common Core, 28, 30–32
  living, of, 1, 48, 115
status, 2, 14, 17, 44, 45, 64, 66, 105
superior, 17
superiority, 2, 3, 5, 6, 7, 10, 66

Tanzania, 42
technology, 24
  communication, 24
  mobile, 58,
  skills, 29
Title IX, 68, 69, 75–77, 78, 79, 80
tradition, 6, 53, 55, 88, 98
traditional, 3, 20, 48–51, 53, 55–56, 59
transnational, 16, 21
transatlantic, 3, 95
Tunisia, 52–53, 54, 55–56
transportation, 9, 13, 16, 20, 22–23, 48, 82

Ubuntu, 3
UC Berkeley, 44
Uganda, 42, 102
United Arab Emirates, 23
United Kingdom, 60, 83, 105
United Nations, 1–2, 22, 25, 28–29, 48, 63, 65–67, 105, 110
  United Nations Decade for Women, 65
United States, 4–5, 10, 14, 16–17, 20–21, 23, 27–28, 30, 32, 33–46 *passim*, 47, 49–50, 55, 58, 60–61, 68–69, 71–84 *passim*, 85–88, 91, 94–96, 100, 103–107, 110–115
Universal Declaration of Human Rights, 21, 63–64, 66

University of Michigan, 35, 39
University of Palmares, 42
"Unveiled Woman," 51, 55
US Supreme Court, 33, 36, 38–39, 40–41, 43–44, 56, 68–69, 90, 100–102
utopia, 20, 22

violence, 10, 60, 66–69, 104–105
  physical, 10, 60, 66–69, 104–105
  sexual, 60–61, 66–69
volence against women, 60–61, 66–69, 78

Wallace v. Jaffree, 102
warfare, 3
welfare, 107, 111–112, 113
white
  Affirmative Action, 45–46
  applicant(s), 40, 43
  boy, 34
  citizens, 108
  communities, 10
  cultural script(s), 4, 43
  elites, 112
  Europeans, 3–5, 15–16
  farmers, 7
  groups, 45
  hue, 6
  individual, 7
  male, 36
  man, 9
  middle class, 34
  people, 6
  person, 9
  population, 35, 45–46, 108
  privilege, 2, 5–9
  race, 6, 9
  racial attitudes, 5
  racial consciousness, 5–6
  racial identity, 5–6
  schools, 10, 34
  skin, 6
  superiority consciousness, 6
  supremacists, 9

supremacy, 10, 15
women, 59
whiteness, 5
whites, 6–7, 10, 15–17, 34, 40, 46–46, 109
white supremacy, 10, 15
Wooden v. the Board of Regents of the University of Georgia, 35, 40–41
World Health Organization (WHO), 67–68
World Systems, 2, 13–17
World Systems Theory, 13–17
worldview(s), 2–5, 9–10, 12–13, 15–17, 48, 50, 53, 91

xenophobia, 5, 17

Year of Women, 64–65

Zorach v. Clauson, 97–98

About the Author

Chinaka Samuel DomNwachukwu is professor and dean of the College of Education at California State University, San Bernardino California. Among his many publications are *Theory and Practice of Multicultural Education*; *An Introduction to Multicultural Education: From Theory to Practice*; and *Multiculturalism: A Shalom Motif for the Christian Community*.

www.ingramcontent.com/pod-product-compliance
Lightning Source LLC
Chambersburg PA
CBHW030114010526
44116CB00005B/244